♥ FOLK ART
FELT

36 Heartfelt Projects
with Creative New Embellishments

by Sandy Belt

Chilton
BOOK COMPANY

FOLK ART FELT
Copyright © 1997 by Landauer Corporation

This book was designed and produced by
Landauer Books
A division of Landauer Corporation
12251 Maffitt Road, Cumming, Iowa 50061

President and Publisher: Jeramy Lanigan Landauer
Editor: Becky Johnston
Art Director: Lyne Neymeyer
Technical Editor: Tricia Coogan
Copy Editor: Joanna Heist
Layout Production: Nicole Bratt
Photography: Lyne Neymeyer; Dennis Kennedy
Cover Photo: Craig Anderson
Technical Illustrators: Tricia Coogan; Roxanne LeMoine; Ruth Schmuff
Creative Associates: Glenda Dawson; Margaret Sindelar
Prepress: Event Graphics
Printed in U.S.A.

Published by Chilton Book Company, Radnor, Pennsylvania

Library of Congress Cataloging-in-Publication Data

Belt, Sandy.
    Folk art felt : 36 heartfelt projects with creative new
  embellishments / Sandy Belt.
      p.   cm.
    Includes index.
    ISBN 0-8019-8943-4
    1. Felt work. 2. Folk art. I. Title.
TT880.B45   1997
746'.0463—dc21   96-51831
                                          CIP

1 2 3 4 5 6 7 8 9 0   6 5 4 3 2 1 0 9 8 7

Introduction

In her delightful folk-art felt book, designer Sandy Belt creates a fabulous collection of 36 fresh new heartfelt projects exclusively for this book.

One of the country's leading designers, award-winning folk artist Sandy Belt has developed new creative ways to embellish easy-to-finish felt. Each chapter opens with a whimsical felt wallhanging reflecting the chapter's theme—home, heart, holidays, family, and friendship. The coordinating sew-simple projects in the chapter provide even more inspiration.

Discover fun wearables, country critters, dressed-up dolls, tree skirt and stockings, pins and a pillow, a hooked table mat, decorative home accents, and much more!

Sandy shows you how to go beyond basic felt with the newest and quickest way to use strips of felted wool for rug hooking projects.

She also tells you how to create soft, richly-textured decorative accents for the home by over-dyeing the all-new wool felt developed by National Nonwovens. The mottled effect found in plant-dyed fabrics is achieved using Dritz cold-water dyes in fun colors such as Koala Brown, Nasturtium, and Sahara Sun.

Sandy then tops it all off with imaginative ways to embellish with tassels and trims from Prym-Dritz, pearl cotton and floss from DMC, elegant silk-embroidery ribbons from YLI, plus buttons, beads, and yo-yos.

To help you experience the fun of working with these new materials and techniques, Sandy provides you with several pages of Tips & Techniques, and an illustrated step-by-step Stitch Guide for embroidering on felt with silk ribbon.

Even if you are a first-time sewer or crafter, you'll be amazed at how quickly and simply you can achieve spectacular results! The fun begins on page 14, appropriately enough, with "A Heartfelt Welcome." Enjoy!

Becky Johnston, *Editor*

Table of Contents

Heartfelt Welcome
Page 14

Just for Kids
Page 42

Harvest Home
Page 66

4

Holiday Spirit
Page 80

Valentine, Be Mine
Page 98

Forever Friends
Page 114

Thanks a Bunch!
Page 127

5

About the Author

♥ ♥ ♥ Sandy Belt's designs have been featured in numerous publications including: Better Homes and Gardens Special Interest Publications' *Christmas Ideas, Country Crafts, Santa Claus,* and *Holiday Crafts; Traditional Home; Michael's Arts & Crafts; Woman's Day Christmas Crafts; Quick and Easy Crafts; Christmas Traditions; Doll Collectors;* and *Teddy Bear and Friends.*

Her patterns are included in collections offered by Indygo Junction and The McCall Pattern Company. In addition, Sandy has created numerous designs for leading manufacturers including YLI, Offray, DMC, Prym-Dritz, National Nonwovens, Zweigart, and Kunin Felt.

Sandy's individually crafted, signed, and dated collector dolls marketed under the Town Folk label are featured in the FolkWorks Gallery in Evanston, Illinois and carried in the gift shop of the Museum of American Folk Art in New York City.

In 1993, Sandy had the privilege of meeting President Clinton at a ceremony honoring entrepreneurs, and presented him with one of her unique dolls.

Sandy Belt's large, close-knit family became the impetus for her surprising career. Raising seven children in a farmhouse near Marquette, Michigan, Sandy and her husband, Tom, a fireman, were struggling to make ends meet. To save money, Sandy taught herself to sew and made all the kid's clothes. A mid-life crisis and help from art appreciators launched her career. And the rest is history!

"THANKS A BUNCH" NOTECARD

The notecard featured here is just a sampling of the treats in store for you on the following pages! (For the full-size pattern, please turn to page 128.) Versatility is a trademark of Sandy Belt's designs—you can adapt them for varied techniques from appliqué to hooking with felted wool (see page 127).

Tips and Techniques

Wool Felt

Most of the projects in this book were made with National Nonwovens felt. I especially like the texture of their 20% and 35% WoolFelt™ after it has been shrunk in the dryer.

Although the manufacturer recommends dry cleaning only, I've broken the rules by pre-shrinking these felts to give them a richer, loftier look and feel.

When I can't find the exact color I want, I like to dye my own colors. I usually begin with National Nonwovens' straw WoolFelt™. I buy it by the yard, cut it into smaller pieces, and dye the pieces with Dritz Cold-Water Dyes. Sometimes I over-dye a colored piece of the felt to create an exciting new shade. I often use tie-dye techniques to dye my felt so the colors are shaded rather than solid. Remember to dry your dyed fabrics in the dryer.

To shrink your wool felt, soak it in hot water; gently squeeze out the excess water; and dry it in a dryer. The dyes will run, so wash and dry each color separately. I don't recommend machine washing. The agitation of your machine will cause the felt to overstretch. However, the heat of your dryer is necessary for the wool to shrink—air-drying would leave the fabric feeling stiff.

Some color may come off onto the drum of your dryer. To protect your next load, either clean the drum between loads, or dry a load of dark color items after each felt load.

I do not recommend hand-washing the finished pieces. Even though the fabrics have been pre-shrunk, some colors will continue to bleed and the felt will continue to shrink. Soiled projects should be dry cleaned only.

I don't like what happens to the texture of felt after it has been pressed. For this reason, I avoid using fusible webs to hold my pieces in place; I use straight pins instead. I prefer the softer look, but to remove wrinkles, hold a steam iron just above the surface of the felt without pressing onto the fabric.

Transfer pens and pencils usually require pressing, so I prefer to hand-print any words or designs that I plan to embroider onto felt with a disappearing-ink marker. If you like working with fusible web or transfer pens, test the results on felt scraps first.

Felt stretches. Steam will remove some puckers caused by stretching.

If you substitute another fabric for the felt animals, you may be disappointed by the finished size. Woven fabric does not stretch like the felt does when the animal is stuffed. If you substitute a woven fabric to make any of my stuffed animals, add an extra ⅛" to ¼" of fabric around any pattern piece that will be stuffed.

Felted Wools

Felted wools were used for the two hooked pieces and can be used in place of felt for many of these projects. Felted wool is made by shrinking a knit or woven wool fabric so the cut edges no longer ravel.

To make your own felted wool, machine-wash and dry any 80%–100% wool fabric. Cut off a piece and if the edges still ravel, shrink the wool again. This process is fun, but can be frustrating. Some fabrics may look far better than you ever anticipated while others may disappoint you. Begin with the color you want to work with or shrink an off-white piece of wool and dye your own colors. Avoid washable wools—they won't shrink. Felted wool fabrics can also be purchased through rug hooking suppliers (see Sources on page 13).

Cutting and Marking Tools

I nearly always cut through one layer of felt at a time. The felt edges will not be turned under so you'll need to work with a sharp pair of scissors to get a good, clean cut. I use embroidery scissors to cut out any tiny inside pieces. A rotary cutter can be used for long straight edges, but the blade must be sharp to avoid stretching the edges. Pinking shears are great for edges that won't be stitched. Some rotary cutters have a pinking blade.

For cleaner cuts, I prefer tracing around my patterns with a water-erasable marker before cutting out the pieces. I then hold the felt in one hand while I cut with the other, feeding the felt into the scissors as I cut. Remove the traced lines as you cut or your pieces will be too large.

My favorite markers are Dritz Mark-B-Gone markers. I use their white-ink marker on dark fabrics and the water-erasable marker for all other colors. Trace lightly; too much pressure can cause the felt to stretch.

Always test the markers on scraps to see how they react with your fabric. The moisture needed to remove the lines will cause some felt colors to bleed. To mark lines that can't be cut off or washed off, try using a disappearing-ink marker.

To save space, only half of some patterns have been given. Instead of cutting the felt on the fold, I prefer to trace my design onto a folded piece of tracing paper. Then I cut out the pattern and unfold the paper for a complete pattern. I trace around the entire pattern piece on my felt and cut through just one layer.

For very large pieces, only diagrams are provided. Their dimensions can be drawn onto your felt using a water-erasable marker and a yardstick, but I prefer working with rulers that were designed to be used with rotary cutters.

Threads

Most of the projects were hand-stitched using DMC pearl cotton threads—the higher the number, the thinner the thread. Pearl cottons are sold in three sizes. I prefer working with size 8 DMC Pearl Cotton. It is sold in 10-gram balls with about 95 yards per ball. This is a great choice for large projects.

Size 5 DMC Pearl Cotton is sold in 10-gram balls with about 53 yards per ball. It is also sold in 5.3-gram skeins with about 27 yards per skein. The skeins are sometimes easier to find than the balls and are a great choice when you're using a variety of colors or when working on small projects. For most of the projects in this book, size 8 and size 5 pearl cottons are interchangeable.

Size 3 DMC Pearl Cotton is sold in 5.6 gram skeins with about 16 yards per skein. This is a much heavier thread and I use it only for special embellishments such as French knots or stem stitches.

I cut my threads about 18" long. Longer lengths can knot and fray. When it appears that an entire piece can be stitched with just one length of thread I will break this rule and use a slightly longer length.

Don't be afraid to experiment with threads. Some of my projects were stitched with 2mm and 4mm silk ribbon. Look for interesting substitutes, such as crochet cotton or a metallic thread, in the cross-stitch or yarn department of your favorite craft store.

Needles

Use a needle with a sharp point and a large enough eye to hold your thread or ribbon. Crewel embroidery and chenille needles work best. I prefer chenille needles because the needle is thicker than others and makes a larger hole for the thread or ribbon to pass through.

Buy an assortment of needles to determine what works best for you. The lower the number, the larger the needle.

Some of my recommendations are based on manufacturer's recommendations, but I often use larger needles when working with felt.

Embroidery Stitches

The stitches I use for most of my projects are very basic and are illustrated on pages 11–13.

Many of the designs require only that you know how to make a simple blanket stitch, a running stitch, a straight stitch, or the irregular straight stitch shown opposite.

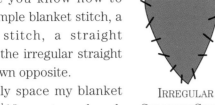

IRREGULAR
STRAIGHT STITCH

I usually space my blanket stitches ¼" apart, and make them ¼" deep. For smaller projects, try spacing ⅛" stitches ⅛" apart, and for larger projects, try spacing ⅜" stitches ⅜" apart. For added interest, try alternating a long stitch with a short stitch, or try spacing every other stitch close to the preceding stitch.

When working with several layers of felt, I prefer stitching only through the next layer if possible. Pulling the thread through more than two layers can be difficult. When attaching buttons, I usually stitch through all layers both to hold the layers together and to better support the weight of the button.

Rug Hooking

Many of the designs are easily adapted for other craft projects. Two of my designs appear in this book as small hooked pieces. The instructions are written with the assumption that you already know how to hook. If not, here are some basics: With one hand, hold your hook above the area to be worked. With the other hand hold

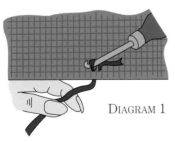

DIAGRAM 1

a strip of wool below the area to be worked. Push the hook between the burlap threads and pull up the end of the wool strip, leaving about a 1"-long tail on top. Push the hook between the next set of burlap threads and pull up a loop.

Checking that the strip lies smooth against the back, continue pulling up loops until only 1" of the strip is left. Make all loops the same height, skipping one or two holes of burlap

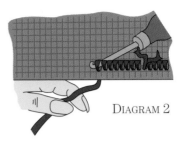

DIAGRAM 2

whenever the loops appear to be too tightly packed. End by pulling up the last 1" to the top. Starting in the last hole worked, add a new strip and continue hooking.

Work outlines and small details first, then fill in large areas. When finished, trim the 1" ends so they are even with the loops. The rows will meld together better if you work in curves rather than straight lines, leaving some space between the rows so the loops are not too tightly packed.

Never carry a strip of wool across the back of your work to fill in a new area with the same color. Always cut the strip and start again in the new spot.

When you are finished, do not leave any loose ends on the back of your work. Always pull the loose ends to the front and trim them to the length of the loops.

**STANDARD PROJECT
SUPPLIES**

Pencil
♥
Tracing paper
♥
Machine-sewing threads
to match fabrics
♥
Sewing machine and standard
sewing supplies
♥
Dressmaker's straight pins
♥
Craft glue
♥
Hot-glue gun
♥

HOW TO USE THE STITCH GUIDE

You'll find that a special feature of the complete how-to instructions for each ribbon-embroidery project is the easy-to-use coded reference guide for stitches, materials, and colors.

Begin by referring to the embroidery pattern that shows the design and position of the stitches. As shown here, the pattern is drawn in full detail with an accompanying code.

The code has three elements: a number in a circle, a capital letter, and a number or series of numbers.

The first element—a number in a circle—indicates the stitch that you will use to make a flower, leaf, or stem.

Note: All the stitches used in a project are identified in the STITCHES box located on the same page as the embroidery pattern. A step-by-step guide to the stitches begins on page 11.

The second element—a capital letter—denotes the width of the thread or ribbon used for that particular stitch.

The third and final element—a number or series of numbers—indicates the ribbon or thread color.

Note: The ribbons and colors are identified in the MATERIALS list that appears with each project.

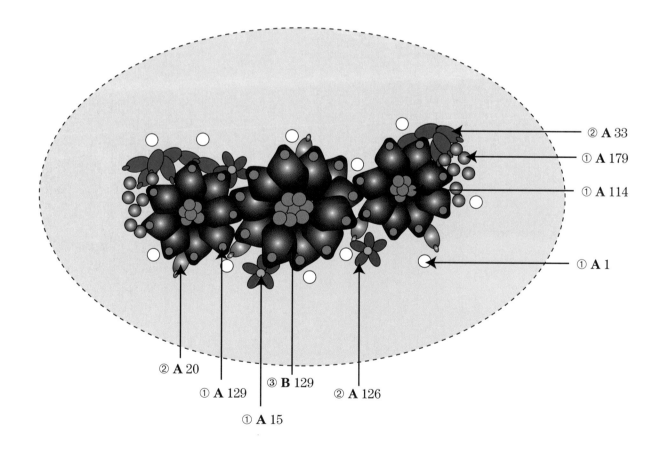

② **A** 33
① **A** 179
① **A** 114
① **A** 1

② **A** 20
① **A** 129
③ **B** 129
② **A** 126
① **A** 15

Stitch Guide

Bullion Stitch

1. Begin by bringing the needle up at A. Put the needle through the fabric at B and then back to A again. Do not pull the needle through the fabric.
2. Keeping the ribbon flat, wrap the tip of the needle evenly until an area is covered approximately equal to the desired length of the stitch.
3. Hold the wraps of ribbon secure with the thumb and forefinger of your left hand. Slowly draw the needle through, until the knot lies flat on the fabric. Insert the needle back through the fabric next to B.

   Note: To make a rose, work a bullion knot wrapping the needle five to nine times. Work two more bullion knots, one above, and one below the first, allowing them to gently surround the center knot.

Buttonhole Stitch / Blanket Stitch

1. To make the stitch, bring your needle and ribbon up through the fabric at A. With your left thumb, hold the ribbon flat against the fabric at point A and to the left. Go down at B and up at C.
2. With the next stitch, point C becomes point A and you repeat the original stitch.

Couching Stitch

This stitch is used to apply ribbon, thread, braid, or other embellishments to the surface of the fabric. A single long stitch is made and then tacked down with another ribbon or thread. The tacking ribbon or thread may be the same color or a contrasting color. The tacking stitch may also be any desired stitch such as a French Knot.

1. The couching stitch is made by bringing the threaded needle up at A and down at B. Pull tacking thread or ribbon tight, thereby holding the decoration to fabric.
2. Repeat the stitch until you have completely attached the decoration.

Cross Stitch

The cross stitch is a series of straight stitches combined to make a pattern of *X*s.

1. Bring your needle and ribbon up at A, down at B, up at C, and down at D.
2. Repeat, making sure that the top stitch goes in the same direction in every *X* you create.

Feather Stitch

Imagine a straight line on the fabric where you are stitching. This imaginary line serves as a guide as you sew individual stitches on either side of the line.

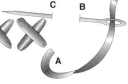

1. Starting at the top of the imaginary line, bring the needle up through the fabric at A and down at B, holding the ribbon loose on top of the fabric with your left thumb to form a loop from A to B. Allow the ribbon to curve gently, but not twist.

   Imaginary line

2. Come up at C, keeping the loop below the needle. This is the point of the *V* formed by the ribbon from A to B.

Stitch Guide

French Knot Stitch

1. Bring the needle and ribbon up at A. Pull the ribbon taut with your left hand. Wrap the ribbon around the needle once, keeping it flat. More wraps will make a larger knot.
2. Insert the needle at B and pull the ribbon so the knot is pushed close to the fabric. Keep the tension even, but do not pull too tightly or you will be unable to pull the needle through the knot and the fabric. If you leave the ribbon too loose an unwanted loop will appear at the knot.
3. Pull the ribbon down at B. Keep holding the ribbon taut until most of the ribbon has been pulled through.

Herringbone Stitch

1. Stitch from left to right, bringing your needle and ribbon up at A.
2. With the ribbon flat, go down at B and up at C in one stitch. Now, cross over the ribbon that runs from A to B and insert your needle at D. Bring your needle up at the next A.
3. Repeat these stitches, forming a series of *X*s or crosses. The location and size of each cross is determined by the distance between B and C and between A and D.

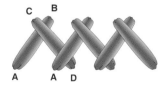

Lazy Daisy Stitch

1. Bring the ribbon up at A. Hold the ribbon flat against the fabric with your thumb while forming the loop. Insert the needle through the fabric at B and bring the needle up at C in the same stitch. Pull the ribbon through, keeping the loop full. Pierce the top edge of the loop at D and pull through, securing the stitch.

Note: Another option for securing the loop of the lazy daisy stitch is a French knot.

Loop Stitch

1. To make this stitch, bring the ribbon up at A. Hold the ribbon to form a loop, with one half of the ribbon on top of the other half of the ribbon. Hold the loop with your left thumb so that the ribbon folds back evenly. Do not have any twist in the ribbon or you will lose the petal effect.
2. Insert the needle at B, pulling the ribbon until it forms the length and appearance you desire.

Note: Make several loop stitches to form flower petals. The center of the flower may be a French knot or a straight stitch. Make either stitch at the base of each petal to secure the petals to the fabric. Another treatment for tiny flowers is to flatten the loop stitch with a French Knot in the center.

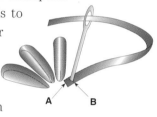

Running Stitch

1. Bring the needle up at A. Insert the needle in and out of the fabric as in general sewing, taking several stitches at the same time.

Satin Stitch

The satin stitch is a series of straight stitches worked side by side to completely cover a specified area. The stitch is most beautiful when it is uniform and smooth.

1. Bring the needle up at A, then down at B. This completes one stitch. Keep the ribbon flat, making sure that each stitch is close to, but not overlapping, the previous stitch.

The distance from A to B is variable for each stitch, depending on the space or the area you need to cover.

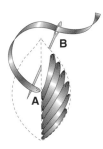

Stem Stitch

This stitch is ideal for outlining large areas.

1. Begin the stitch by bringing your needle up at A. Hold the ribbon flat on the fabric with your thumb to either side of the stem line. Regardless of which side you choose to begin your stitching, remember to stay on the same side with the rest of your stitches.

2. Before pulling the A to B stitch flat to the fabric, bring the needle up at C. Tighten the stitch. C now becomes A for the next stitch. Continue, slightly overlapping the previous stitch until the desired length of the stem is reached.

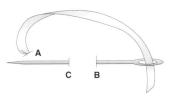

SOURCES

Brass Charms: To locate the nearest retailer write: Creative Beginnings, 475 Morro Bay Boulevard, Morro Bay, CA 93442.

Chainette: Look for Chainette trim wherever Offray ribbons are sold. To locate the nearest retailer write: C. M. Offray and Son, Inc., 261 Madison Avenue, New York, NY 10016.

Cold-Water Dyes, Mark-B-Gone Markers, Needles, Drapery and Upholstery Trims: Look for the recommended dyes, markers, needles, plastic rings, fringes, and trims wherever Prym-Dritz products are sold. To locate the nearest retailer write: Prym-Dritz Corporation, Spartanburg, SC 29304.

Felts and Felt Vest: Look for National Nonwovens WoolFelt™ and their vest at your favorite fabric store. To locate the nearest retailer write or call: National Nonwovens, P.O. Box 150, Easthampton, MA 01027; 1-800/333-3469.

Felted Wools and Rug Hooking Supplies: For a free brochure listing kits, rug hooking supplies, and hand-dyed felted wools send a self-addressed, stamped business-size envelope to: Moondance Color Company, 622 Spencer Road, Oakham, MA 01068. To receive a color card containing actual samples of the hand-dyed wools, include $2.

Frames, Mirror, and Keepsake Box: Look for these products at your favorite needlework or frame shop. To locate the nearest retailer write or call: East Side

Mouldings, 745 East Main Street, Ephrata, PA 17522; 800/840-6077. The mirror on page 18 is their 6" x 6" Wee Mirror (black schoolhouse); the frame on page 28 is their 23" x 11" (2100-BK) custom double frame; and the green box on page 127 is their 6" x 6" Americana Box (item 3400G). A green 6" x 6" frame can be substituted for the box (item 3300G). Other colors are available.

Pearl Cottons, Embroidery Floss, and Metallic Threads: Look for DMC threads at your favorite craft or needlework shop. To locate the nearest retailer write: DMC Corporation, Port Kearney Building 10, South Kearny, NJ 07032.

Shaker Pincushion and Shaker Sisters Oval Sewing Box: Look for these products at your favorite needlework shop. To locate the nearest retailer write: Sudberry House, P.O. Box 895, Old Lyme, CT 06371.

Silk Ribbons: Look for YLI silk ribbons at your favorite craft or needlework shop. To locate the nearest retailer write or call: YLI Corporation, P.O. Box 109, Provo, UT 84603; 1-800/854-1932

Tulip Paints: Look for Tulip paints at your favorite craft shop. To locate the nearest retailer write: Tulip, 24 Prime Park Way, Natick, MA 01760.

Vest Pattern: The pattern for the child's vest shown on page 51 is Indygo Junction's "It's a Small World" multi-size vest pattern (No. IJ447). To order by mail or locate the nearest retailer call: 913/341-5559.

A Heartfelt Welcome

For a heartfelt welcome, grace your home or gift a friend with folk art straight from the heart!

As it fast becomes a decorating style in its own right, folk blends the best of country and rustic antiquity as it opens up a world of warm relaxed comfort for those who appreciate the simple pleasures of life.

To get started, simply combine a palette of traditional colors that captures the vim and vigor of colonial America with a collection of equally homespun fabrics—flannel, wool and felt.

With the focus on easy-to-finish felt, choose from a variety of projects you can create in less time than you've ever imagined!

Shown here and on the following pages, you'll find folk art felt on everything from the featured wallhanging, *below,* to Homespun Hannah, a star-spangled primitive rag doll who proudly reflects our American heritage.

Topped off with bits of lace, snippets of ribbon, and one-of-a-kind treasures from the button box, these charming folk art delights are sure to win your heart.

"WELCOME HOME" WALLHANGING

Wallhanging is 16¼" high x 26⅞" wide

For information about materials, tools, techniques, and stitches, read "Tips and Techniques" starting on page 7.

Materials

⅝ yard of champagne or straw wool felt for the backing and letters

♥

½ yard of black wool felt for the background and tree trunk

♥

One 9" x 12" piece of loden or blue spruce wool felt for the tree top, ground, and trim

♥

One 9" x 12" piece of burgundy or plum wool felt for the hearts, roof, door, and chimney

♥

One 9" x 12" piece of white wool felt for the house

♥

One 9" x 12" piece of old gold wool felt for the sun and rays

♥

One 11" square of cotton fabric for the heart

♥

Size 8 DMC pearl cotton: one ball of black (No. 310)

♥

No. 2 crewel embroidery needle or No. 22 chenille needle

♥

Several ½" or ¾" plastic rings

♥

Mark-B-Gone marking pens

♥

Prepare Pieces

1. Referring to the diagrams on page 30, trace red portion of backing/background pattern pieces onto the bottom half of a sheet of tracing paper. Shift the tracing paper so the red A's and B's match with the black A's and B's, and trace black portion of pattern. In the same way, trace patterns on page 31, joining C to C, and D to D. Join these two sections to form a complete pattern.

2. Trace the large heart pattern on page 33. Cut out.

3. Referring to diagrams on page 31, cut backing from champagne or straw felt.

4. Referring to diagrams on page 31, trim backing/background pattern along short dashed lines and use to cut background on fold of black felt. With black still folded, cut the large heart out of the background, positioning the pattern about 1" above bottom straight edge.

5. Referring to diagrams with the full-size patterns on pages 30–31, trace all the remaining design pieces. The dashed lines show where pieces are either underlapped or overlapped. Cut out.

6. Referring to materials list for suggested colors and to diagrams for numbers, trace around remaining patterns on felt. Cut out, removing traced lines as you cut. Use embroidery scissors to cut out inside portion of letter *O*.

A Heartfelt Welcome

Years ago, I discovered how easy it is to achieve a rustic, folk art feeling using felt. I've continued my love affair with felt by creating soft, richly-textured decorative accents for the home by over-dyeing the new wool felt.

Stitch Design

1. Center the 11" square of fabric on the backing as seen in the diagram on page 31. Pin the black background piece on top of the backing, adjusting the fabric layer so it shows through the heart without extending outside the edges of the background piece. Pin fabric in place.

2. Use black pearl cotton to blanket-stitch the outer edge of background to backing, leaving edges of cutout heart unstitched for now. Use black pearl cotton to outline the jagged edge of backing with long running stitches, stitching about ¼" in from the edge.

3. Smooth out the fabric layer behind the heart cutout. Use black pearl cotton and a long running stitch to hold it in place, stitching on the fabric about ⅛" in from the edge of the black felt.

4. Place the ground piece at the bottom of the fabric heart, slipping it under the felt cutout so black felt overlaps it at the dashed lines. Slip the house and door and tree trunk under the ground piece at the dashed lines. Pin in place.

5. Arrange and pin tree top so it overlaps tree trunk at the dashed line. Arrange and pin roof so it overlaps house at dashed line; slip chimney under roof at dashed line. Arrange and pin the sun and rays.

6. Use black pearl cotton for all stitching. Always sew through the next layer of felt or fabric only. Do not try to stitch through all layers. Attach rays with running stitches, and sun with blanket stitch. Attach house, door, roof, and chimney with blanket stitch. Attach small heart with irregular straight stitches. Attach tree trunk with running stitch, and tree top and top edge of ground with blanket stitch.

7. Using black pearl cotton, blanket-stitch all the exposed edges of black felt surrounding fabric heart.

8. Referring to photo for placement, arrange and pin all remaining design pieces to top of felt background.

9. Using black pearl cotton, blanket-stitch all remaining pieces in place.

Finish Wallhanging

1. For hangers, hand-sew several small plastic rings to the backing, evenly distributing the weight.

FRAMED MIRROR

Frame is 23" high x 7⅛" wide with
a 9" x 6" mirror.
Each design fits a 6" x 6" opening

For information about materials, tools, techniques, and stitches, read "Tips and Techniques" starting on page 7.

Materials

¼ yard or two 9" x 12" pieces of black wool felt for the background

❤

One 9" x 12" piece of white or straw wool felt for the house, moon, and bottom heart

❤

One 9" x 12" piece of burgundy or plum wool felt for the roof, tiny heart, door, top heart, and berries

❤

One 9" x 12" piece of loden wool felt for the tree, ground, and trim

❤

One 9" x 12" piece of light brown or oakwood wool felt for the tree trunk

❤

Size 8 DMC pearl cotton: one ball of black (No. 310)

❤

Size 5 DMC pearl cotton: one skein of gold (No. 783)

❤

No. 22 chenille needle

❤

Wee Mirror (see Sources on page 127)

❤

Two 6" x 6" pieces of cardboard

❤

Wire brads or glazier points for framing

❤

Sawtooth hanger

❤

Prepare Pieces

1. Referring to the diagrams and full-size patterns on page 34, trace individual pieces. Cut out.

2. Referring to materials list for suggested colors and to diagrams for numbers, trace around patterns on felt. Cut out. For backgrounds, cut two 8" x 8" black felt squares.

Stitch Design No. 1

1. On the center of one 8" x 8" background piece, arrange Design No. 1 as seen on pattern. Pin in place.

2. Using black pearl cotton for all stitching, attach top heart to bottom heart with irregular straight stitches. Always sew through next layer of felt only. Do not try to stitch through all layers.

3. Blanket-stitch bottom heart to the background. Attach trim with irregular straight stitches.

4. Attach berries as shown, finishing the center of each with a French knot.

Stitch Design No. 2

1. On the center of one 8" x 8" background piece, arrange Design No. 2 as seen on pattern. The dashed lines show where pieces are overlapped. Pin in place.

2. Using black pearl cotton, attach moon, house, tree trunk, ground, tree top, and small heart with irregular straight stitches. Blanket-stitch door and roof in place. Always sew through the next layer of felt only. Do not try to stitch through all the layers.

3. For stars, thread needle with gold No. 5 pearl cotton. Referring to pattern for position, embroider each star as shown, bringing needle to front at odd numbers and to back at even numbers.

Frame Designs

1. Wrap each stitched design around a 6" x 6" piece of heavy cardboard. Wrap Design No. 1 so the excess ½" on each side of green trim folds to the back. Place designs in frame, holding in place with either wire brads or glazier points.

2. Attach sawtooth hanger.

HOOKED WOOL TABLE MAT

Rug is 8½" high x 11¾" wide

For information about materials, tools, techniques, and stitches, read "Tips and Techniques" starting on page 7 which includes rug hooking techniques.

For information on dyed pre-felted wools see Sources on page 13.

Note: A slice of dyed felted wool measures 6½" x 15½".

Materials

¼ yard of black dyed felted flannel-weave wool for the background

One slice of mottled green dyed felted flannel-weave wool for the trim and vine

One slice of red dyed felted flannel-weave wool for the top heart, large berries, and small berries

Felted flannel-weave wool: one slice each or scraps of golden tan for the bottom heart, tan for the branch, and white for the dove

One 16" x 16" piece of Angus burlap (do not use a decorator burlap)

One 9" x 12" piece of tracing paper

Heat-transfer pen or pencil

Rug hooking frame or 14" quilter's hoop

Rug hook

1½ yards of rug-binding (twill) tape

Matching carpet thread

Carpet needle

Prepare Pieces

1. Fold tracing paper in half. Matching fold of paper to fold line of background pattern on page 35, trace background pattern onto paper. Cut out and unfold paper for a complete pattern.

2. Center tracing paper pattern over heart and dove patterns on page 35, and trace entire design, including trim and berries. Turn paper over and trace trim and berries on opposite side of heart to complete the design.

Hook Design

1. To prevent fraying, zigzag-stitch or overcast the edges of burlap.

2. On back of tracing paper, retrace design with transfer pen or pencil. Following manufacturer's instructions transfer design to center of burlap.

3. Place design in quilt hoop, or attach to rug frame.

4. Cut the wools into ³⁄₁₆"-wide strips, carefully cutting along the weave of the wool. Always cut along the length of the fabric rather than across the width.
   On a strip cutting machine, use a No. 6 cutter.

5. Hook the design as drawn, referring to materials list and photo for colors. Outline dove's wing with black.

6. Check for gaps, filling in as needed.

Finish Table Mat

1. Remove table mat from frame. Block as needed. Trim off excess burlap, leaving about a 1" seam allowance.

2. Pre-shrink the rug-binding tape, dyeing it to match the background color if desired.

A Heartfelt Welcome

3. With the table mat turned right side up, lay the rug tape on top of the seam allowance, cutting one long edge of the tape right next to hooked edge. With matching carpet thread and a carpet needle, hand-sew tape in place.

4. Leaving some excess for turning under the ends, cut tape. Turn under the ends so they butt up against each other and hand-stitch in place.

5. Turn rug tape to back and hand sew in place, clipping into burlap seam every few inches so piece lays flat.

My friend Christine Oliver, a rug-hooking expert, used her own hand-dyed, pre-felted wool to create this charming hooked wool table mat inspired by my original design.

"ENTER MY HEART" DOOR DECORATION
Sign is 14" high x 8" wide

For information about materials, tools, techniques, and stitches, read "Tips and Techniques" starting on page 7.

Materials
½ yard or one 12" x 18" piece of loden or blue spruce wool felt for the lettering and trim

♥

½ yard or one 12" x 18" piece of champagne or straw wool felt for the center heart

♥

½ yard or one 12" x 18" piece of black wool felt for the backing

♥

One 9" x 12" piece of burgundy or plum wool felt for the small hearts

♥

Size 8 DMC pearl cotton: one ball of very light tan (No. 738)

♥

No. 2 crewel embroidery needle or No. 22 chenille needle

♥

A total of 16 tan buttons varying in size from ⅜" to 1⅛"

♥

Two ½" or ¾" plastic rings; or 1 yard of any width ribbon plus matching thread and hand-sewing needle

♥

Mark-B-Gone marking pens

♥

Prepare Pieces
1. Referring to the diagrams and full-size patterns on pages 36–37, trace the individual pattern pieces, matching A to A and B to B to complete larger pieces; cut out.
2. Referring to materials list for suggested colors and to diagrams for numbers, trace around patterns on felt; cut out. Use embroidery scissors to cut out inside portion of letter *R*.

Stitch Design
1. Pin center heart on top of backing. Pin trim on each side of center heart, overlapping its edges. Arrange and pin lettering as seen on pattern.
2. Use tan pearl cotton for all stitching. Always sew through next layer of felt only. Do not try to stitch through all layers. Blanket-stitch letters to center heart, leaving cutout section of the letter *R* unstitched.
3. Blanket-stitch outer edges of trim to backing and inside edges of trim to center heart.
4. Arrange and pin four small hearts as seen on pattern; blanket-stitch in place.
5. Referring to photo, use pearl cotton to sew one button to center of each scallop on trim.

Finish Door Decoration
1. To hang sign, hand-sew one or two small plastic rings to backing using thread or pearl cotton.
2. If preferred, omit rings and cut two 18"-long pieces of any width ribbon. Tie two ribbons together, making a bow. Pin untied ends to back of sign, and trim length as needed; hand-sew to backing with matching thread.

I enjoy sorting through my button box for just the right buttons. Here I used assorted brown and tan one-of-a-kind beauties as accents on the scalloped border.

HOMESPUN HANNAH
Doll is 19" tall

For information about materials, tools, techniques, and stitches, read "Tips and Techniques" starting on page 7.

Materials

⅓ yard of brown fabric for the body, arms

❤

⅛ yard of red striped fabric for the legs

❤

⅛ yard of blue striped fabric for the dress

❤

¼ yard of patriotic blue print for the dress

❤

¼ yard of plaid fabric for the dress

❤

⅜ yard of checked print for the pantaloons

❤

One 9" x 12" piece of either beige, champagne, or straw felt for the apron

❤

Scraps or one 9" x 12" square each of denim or royal blue, antique or old gold, and burgundy felt for the apron

❤

Size 5 DMC pearl cotton: black (No. 310)

❤

Size 8 or 5 DMC pearl cotton: dark beige (No. 642)

❤

No. 22 chenille needle

❤

Doll needle

❤

Pearl buttons: two ⅜" two-hole buttons for eyes; one ⁵⁄₁₆" two-hole button and one ¾" four-hole button for center of star; three two- or four-hole buttons for apron in sizes from ⅜" to ⅝"

❤

Polyester stuffing

❤

Mark-B-Gone marking pens: white ink and disappearing-ink

❤

Doll

1. Trace full-size body and arm patterns from page 39 onto tracing paper; cut out.
2. With white marker, trace around body pattern on wrong side of folded brown fabric as seen in Diagram 1. Leaving about 1 inch between pieces to allow for seam allowances, trace two arms.

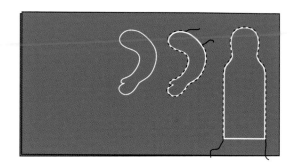

DIAGRAM 1

3. Leaving openings as marked, use a tiny straight stitch to machine-sew on traced lines, beginning and ending all seams with a backstitch. To prevent seams from popping, stitch again, on top of first round of stitches.
4. Cut out pieces, leaving a ¼" seam allowance. Cut unstitched edge at bottom of body on traced line. Clip curves and turn each piece right side out. Press. Referring to patterns, use white marker to mark dots on body and on each side of arms. Insert stuffing. Turn in raw edges and hand-sew openings closed.
5. For face, cut nose from burgundy or overdyed red felt. Referring to pattern and using black pearl cotton, attach nose with running stitches, attach button eyes and embroider mouth.
6. For hair, thread chenille needle with two strands of black pearl cotton. Insert needle on one side of the seam along the top of the head and bring needle out on the other side of the seam. Cut thread, leaving 2" tails on each side of seam. Tie

ends together with a double knot. Continue to add hair along the curve of the head in the same way.

7. Thread doll needle with black pearl cotton and knot the end. Insert needle at dot on one side of body and come out at dot on opposite side of body. Making certain that the thumb points upward, insert needle through one arm at dots and go back through arm a short distance from dots. Next, draw needle back through body, coming out at starting point, and add the second arm. Bring needle back through arm a short distance from dot and tie off thread at starting point.

8. For legs, cut two 2¾" x 12" strips from the red striped fabric. With the right sides together, fold each strip in half lengthwise. Transfer foot pattern to bottom edge of each folded strip.

9. Sew legs as shown in diagram on page 39. Trim off excess fabric. Turn each leg right side out and insert stuffing. Turn in raw edges and hand-stitch legs to bottom of body with toes pointing forward.

Clothing

1. For the pantaloons, cut two 8" x 13" pieces from checked print. Referring to Diagram 2, stitch pieces, right sides together, at side seams. Mark a 9¼" inseam in the center of the unit; sew inseam. Slit open along solid line. Clip curves and turn right side out.

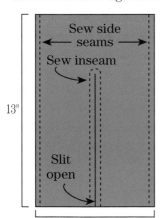

Sew side seams

Sew inseam

Slit open

13"

8"

DIAGRAM 2

2. Press under a ½" hem at waistline and at ankles. Thread embroidery or chenille needle with either two strands of size 8 or one strand of size 5 dark beige pearl cotton. Dress doll and hand-sew a running stitch around waistline, starting and ending stitching at center front and leaving a long tail at each end. Pull gathers to fit doll; tie bow with a double knot. Hand-gather bottom of each leg in the same way.

3. For the dress, cut two sleeves from blue patriotic print and two dress bodices from plaid. Cut two 5½" x 8½" pieces of blue patriotic print and two 3" x 8½" pieces of blue striped fabric. Referring to Diagram 3, sew each blue piece to the bottom of a bodice piece and each striped piece to the bottom of the blue piece.

Sleeve · **Sleeve**

Front of dress

5½" x 8½" **piece**

3½" x 8½" **piece**

DIAGRAM 3

4. Referring to Diagram 3, sew a sleeve to each side of one bodice top; then, sew the opposite side of each sleeve to the remaining bodice top in the same way. Fold dress, right sides together, at sleeves; sew underarm and side seams.

5. Press in ½" hems at bottom of dress and at neckline. Press in ⅜" hems at ends of sleeves. Thread needle with a single strand of dark beige pearl cotton and hand-sew hem at bottom of skirt with a long running stitch about ⅜" above fold. Thread needle with either two strands of size 8 pearl cotton or a single strand of size 5 for neckline and sleeves. Finish sleeves same as for pantaloons. Gather neckline, threading the ends through holes of a large pearl button at center front. Tie bow with a double knot.

6. Referring to diagrams and full-size patterns on page 38, cut felt pieces for apron. Referring to Diagram 4, pin flag pieces onto apron, positioning the blue piece ⅞" below the top 3" edge. Attach blue piece and stripes with a running stitch and single strands of dark beige pearl cotton. Attach star with irregular straight stitches.

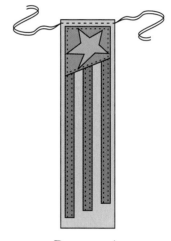

DIAGRAM 4

7. Sew a large button in the center of the star, using the same stitch pattern used on the doll's eyes. In the same way, attach a small button on top of this button. Attach a button to the bottom of each stripe.

8. For apron ties, thread needle with a long, double strand of dark beige pearl cotton. Fold under top edge ½" and sew with a running stitch, leaving long tails at each end. Tie the apron around the doll's waist.

HANGING HEARTS

Each heart is 3¾" high x 3⅜" wide

For information about materials, tools, techniques, and stitches, read "Tips and Techniques" starting on page 7.

Materials

¼ yard or four 9" x 12" pieces of burgundy, plum or overdyed red wool felt for the hearts

♥

¼ yard of small checked cotton fabric in a contrasting color for the letters

♥

Size 5 DMC pearl cotton: one skein of black (No. 310)

♥

No. 22 chenille needle

♥

2 to 4 yards of any width ribbon that coordinates with the fabrics; or several ribbons in a variety of lengths, colors, and widths

♥

Threads to match ribbon, and hand-sewing needle

♥

Tree branch measuring about 3' long x ¾" to 1½" thick

♥

Prepare Pieces

1. From full-size patterns on page 40, trace one large heart on solid lines, one medium heart on dashed lines, and one of each letter, using the small heart for the letter O. Cut out.
2. Trace around large heart 14 times on front of burgundy, plum, or overdyed red felt. Cut out hearts, removing traced lines as you cut. Set aside seven hearts.
3. Trace a letter in the center of each of the remaining seven hearts, spelling out the word WELCOME. With embroidery scissors, carefully cut out each letter right on traced lines.
4. On front of small checked fabric, trace around medium heart seven times. Cut out on traced lines.

Stitch Design

1. With the right sides up, pin one checked heart in the center of each solid felt heart. Pin hearts with cutouts, right side up, on top of checked hearts.
2. Using black pearl cotton for all stitching, blanket-stitch the edges of front and back hearts together.
3. Blanket-stitch around edges of letters, sewing top layer of felt to fabric layer without stitching through back of hearts.

Finish Sign

1. To hang sign, cut seven pieces of ribbon from 10" to 18" long. Fold each piece in half to form a loop and hand-sew the ends to the back of a heart.

FRAMED WELCOME

Frame is 11" high x 23" wide with a 7½" x 19⅛" opening.

For information about materials, tools, techniques, and stitches, read "Tips and Techniques" starting on page 7.

Materials

¼ yard or one 12" x 18" piece of black wool felt for the background

♥

Two 9" x 12" pieces of straw or champagne wool felt for the lettering

♥

One 9" x 12" piece of loden or blue spruce wool felt for the leaves

♥

One 9" x 12" piece or scrap of burgundy or plum wool felt for the heart

♥

⅜ yard or one 12" x 24" piece of plaid cotton fabric for backing

♥

Size 5 DMC pearl cotton: black (No. 310)

♥

Size 5 DMC pearl cotton: avocado green (No. 935)

♥

Size 3 DMC pearl cotton: dark red (No. 498)

♥

No. 20 and No. 22 chenille needles

♥

Custom-made double frame: 23" x 11" black frame with 19½" x 7¾" onion-color frame for inside (see Sources on page 13)

♥

Batting and heavy cardboard to fit frame

♥

Wire brads or glazier points for framing

♥

Sawtooth hanger

♥

Prepare Pieces

1. Referring to the diagrams and full-size patterns on pages 40–41, trace the individual pattern pieces, matching A to A and B to B to complete background piece. Cut out.

2. Referring to materials list for suggested colors and to the diagrams for numbers, trace around the patterns on felt. Notice that the edges of the black wool felt background are irregular, not smooth. Cut out.

Stitch Design

1. Pin felt background in the center of a 12" x 24" piece of plaid fabric. Referring to the full-size patterns on pages 40–41 for position, pin letters and leaves to background. Pin small heart in center of larger heart for letter *O*. The dashed lines show where pieces overlap.

2. Thread a No. 22 chenille needle with black pearl cotton. Use irregular straight stitches to attach the letters and leaves, always sewing through the next layer of the felt or fabric only. Do not try to stitch through all layers.

3. Use black pearl cotton to blanket-stitch background edges to fabric.

Add Embellishments

1. Use a disappearing-ink or water-erasable marker to draw in vines. This can be done freehand using the full-size patterns on pages 40–41 as a guide. The lines do not have to be drawn with precision. The vines should appear to wrap around the letters.

2. Thread a No. 22 chenille needle with avocado green pearl cotton. Embroider vines with stem stitches (also called outline stitch).

3. Thread a No. 20 chenille needle with dark red pearl cotton. Referring to patterns for position, stitch a French knot at each red dot for berries.

Frame Design

1. Cut a piece of heavy cardboard to fit behind frame opening. Cut a piece of batting to fit on top of cardboard. Place batting on top of cardboard and center stitched piece on top of batting.

2. Wrap excess fabric to back of cardboard so design on front is smooth and taut. Insert stitchery behind frame opening; secure in place with either wire brads or glazier points. Finish back as desired.

3. Attach sawtooth hanger.

I find it easy to whip up a warm welcome in a weekend by first selecting the size and shape of frame that best fits my wall. Choosing from among the new frames custom-made to accommodate stitchery, I then adjust the design to fit the frame.

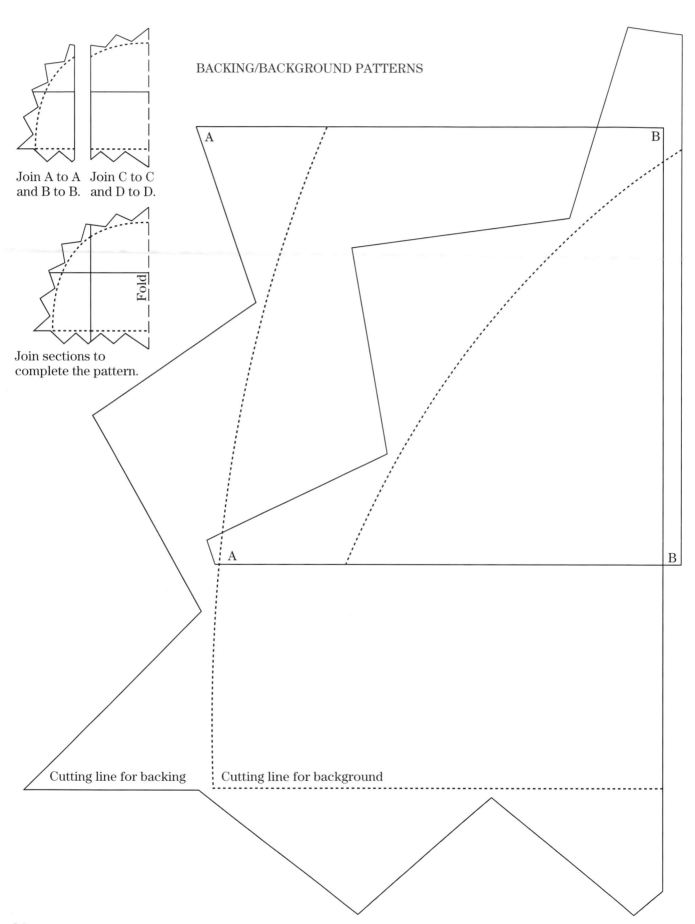

BACKING/BACKGROUND PATTERNS

Join A to A Join C to C
and B to B. and D to D.

Join sections to
complete the pattern.

Fold

A

B

A

B

Cutting line for backing   Cutting line for background

BACKING/BACKGROUND PATTERNS

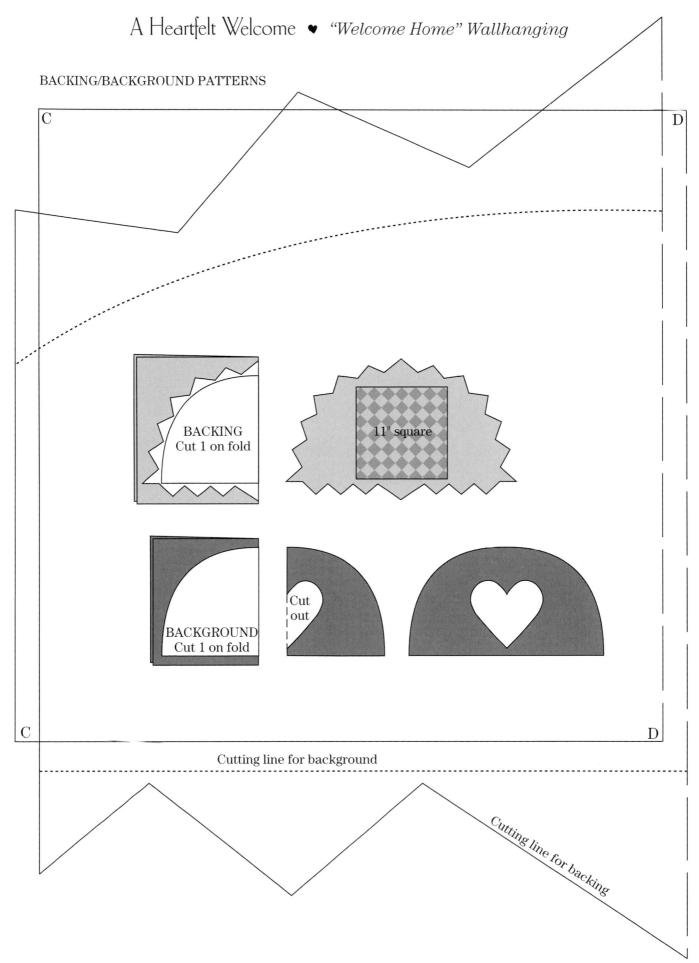

C   D

BACKING
Cut 1 on fold

11" square

BACKGROUND
Cut 1 on fold

Cut out

C   D

Cutting line for background

Cutting line for backing

LETTERS W & E
Cut 2 each
(For M, turn one W
upside down.)

LETTERS L, C, & O
Cut 1 each

BORDER
HEART NO. 1
Cut 2

BORDER
HEART NO.2
Cut 2

BORDER
HEART NO.3
Cut 2

Cut
out

TREE
TOP
Cut 1

TREE
TRUNK
Cut 1

GROUND
Cut 1

TRIM
Cut 1
Cut 1 in
reverse

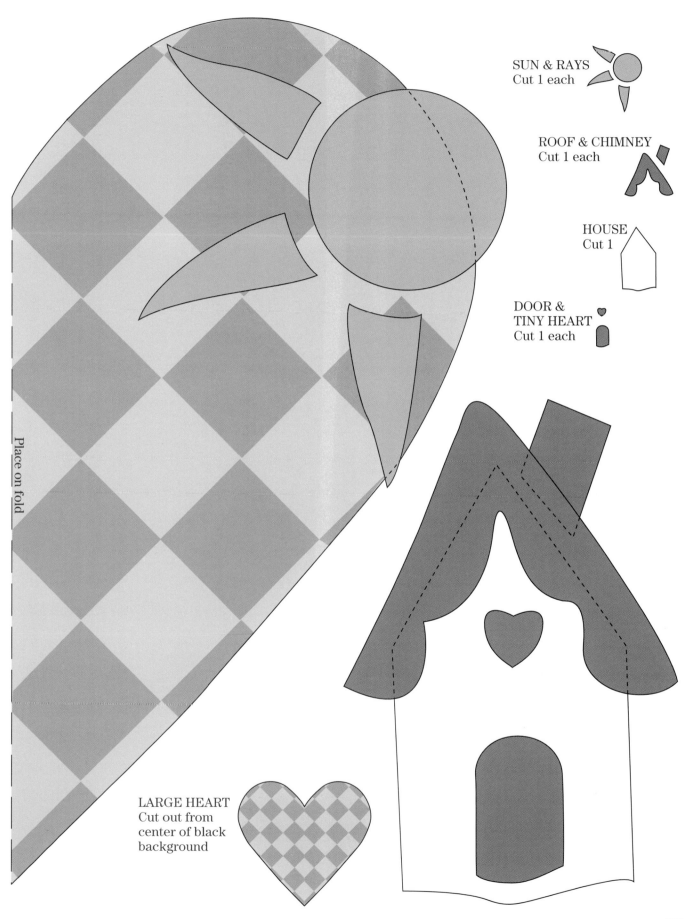

SUN & RAYS
Cut 1 each

ROOF & CHIMNEY
Cut 1 each

HOUSE
Cut 1

DOOR &
TINY HEART
Cut 1 each

Place on fold

LARGE HEART
Cut out from
center of black
background

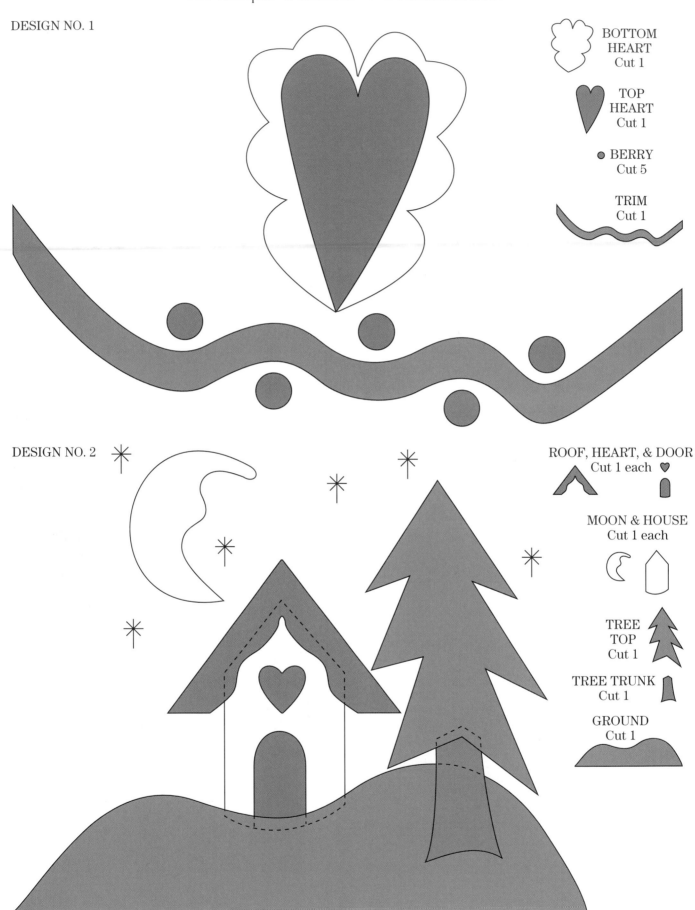

DESIGN NO. 1

BOTTOM
HEART
Cut 1

TOP
HEART
Cut 1

● BERRY
Cut 5

TRIM
Cut 1

DESIGN NO. 2

ROOF, HEART, & DOOR
Cut 1 each ♥

MOON & HOUSE
Cut 1 each

TREE
TOP
Cut 1

TREE TRUNK
Cut 1

GROUND
Cut 1

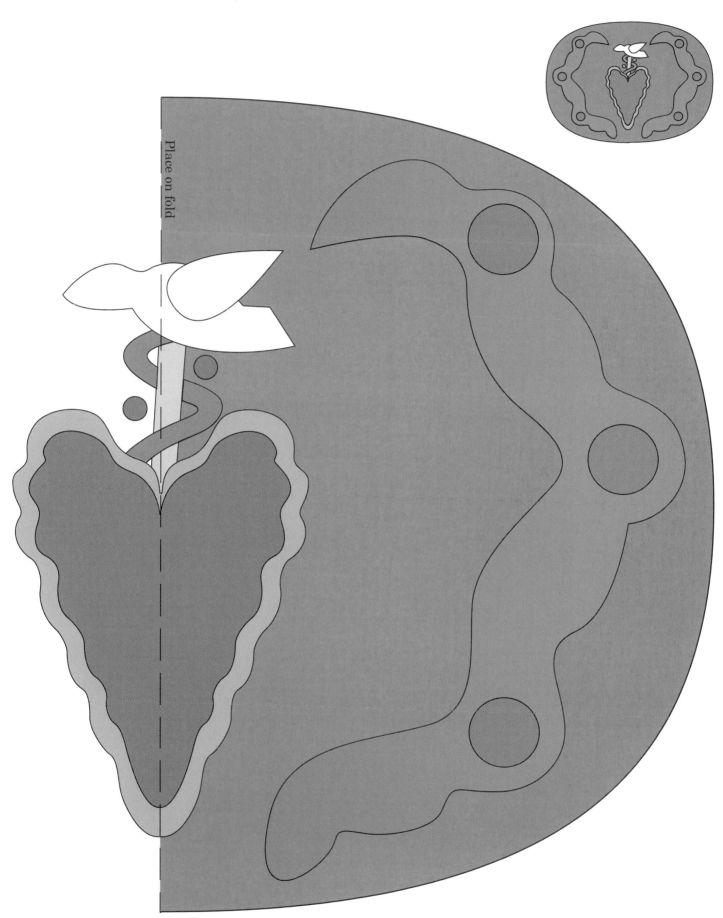

Place on fold

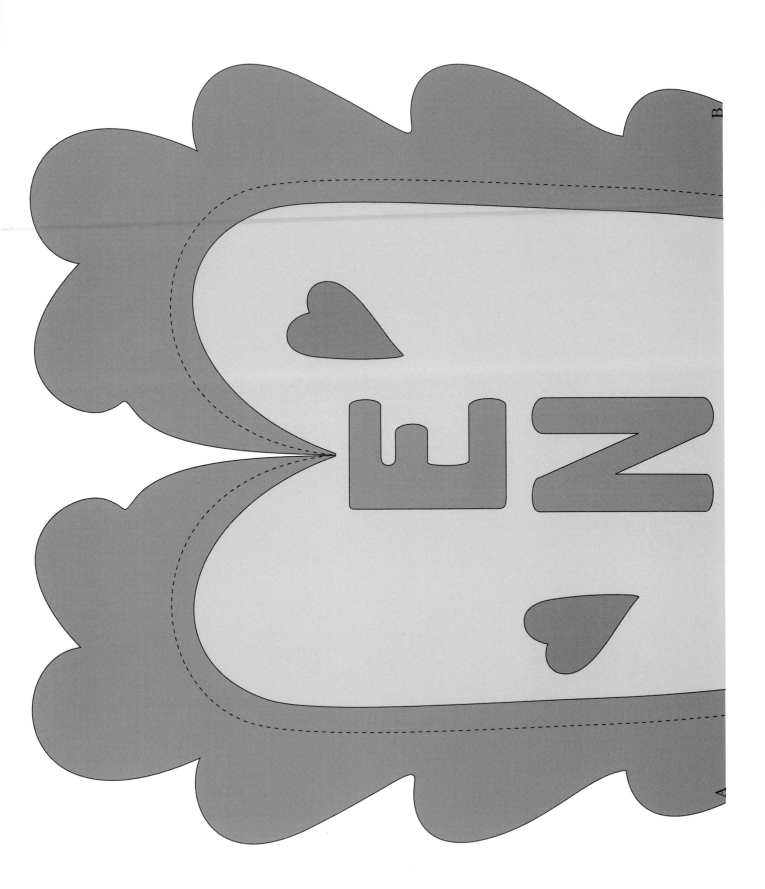

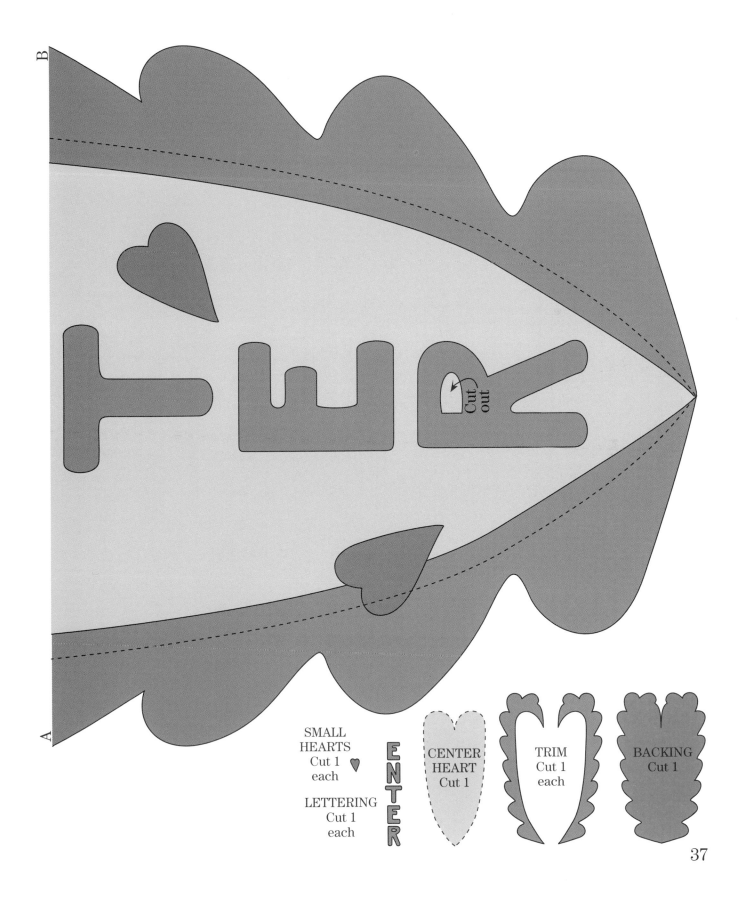

SMALL
HEARTS
Cut 1 ♥
each

LETTERING
Cut 1
each

ENTER

CENTER
HEART
Cut 1

TRIM
Cut 1
each

BACKING
Cut 1

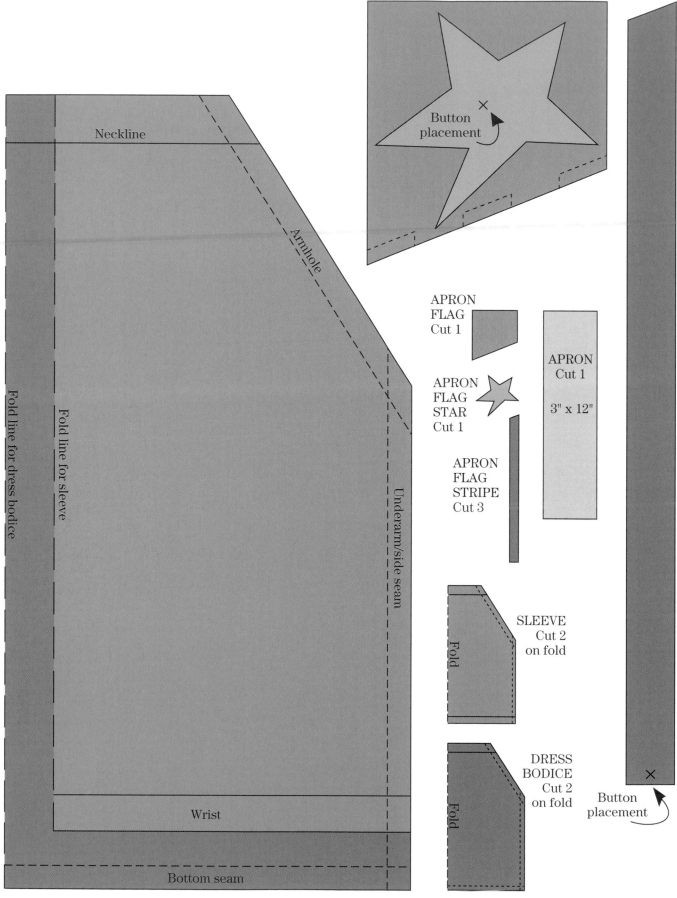

Button placement

Neckline

Armhole

Underarm/side seam

Fold line for dress bodice

Fold line for sleeve

APRON
FLAG
Cut 1

APRON
FLAG
STAR
Cut 1

APRON
FLAG
STRIPE
Cut 3

APRON
Cut 1

3" x 12"

SLEEVE
Cut 2
on fold

Fold

DRESS
BODICE
Cut 2
on fold

Fold

Button
placement

Wrist

Bottom seam

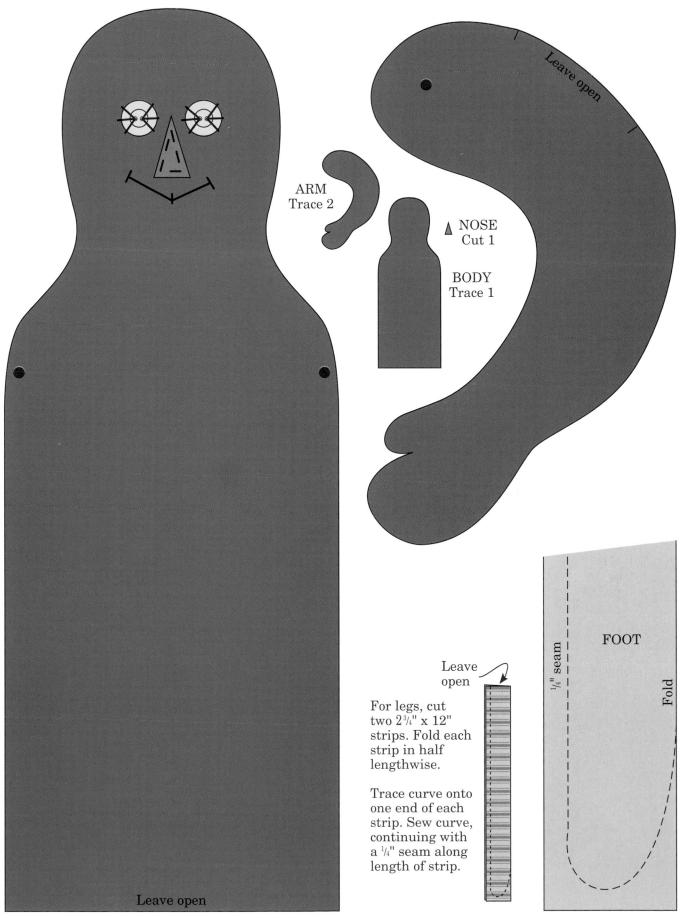

ARM
Trace 2

▲ NOSE
Cut 1

BODY
Trace 1

Leave open

Leave open

Leave
open

For legs, cut
two 2³⁄₄" x 12"
strips. Fold each
strip in half
lengthwise.

Trace curve onto
one end of each
strip. Sew curve,
continuing with
a ¹⁄₄" seam along
length of strip.

FOOT

¹⁄₄" seam

Fold

Cut out

BACK
HEARTS
Cut 7
from felt

CENTER
HEARTS
Cut 7 from
cotton print

FRONT
HEARTS
Cut 7
from felt
(Cut out
one letter from
center of each heart.)

Stem-stitch
vines

French
knots

B

A

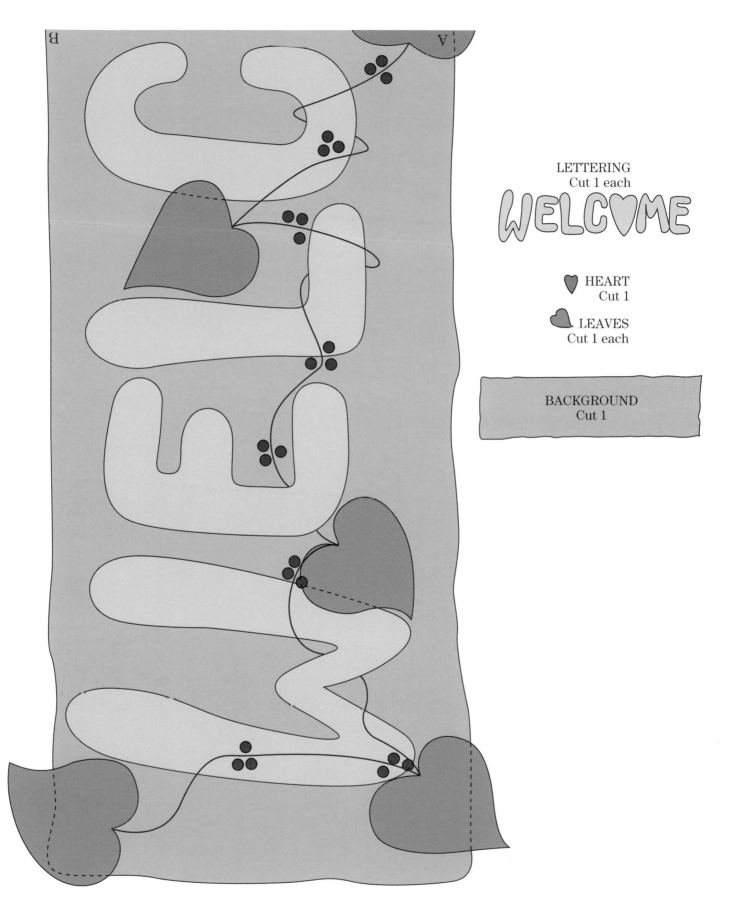

LETTERING
Cut 1 each

HEART
Cut 1

LEAVES
Cut 1 each

BACKGROUND
Cut 1

Just for Kids

The first verse of an enduring holiday favorite, the beloved Christmas carol, "Silent Night," closes tenderly with the phrase "sleep in heavenly peace." Used as the theme for a collection of heavenly felt and fabric projects "just for kids," it becomes a year-round lullaby!

Start with the yo-yo bordered wallhanging, *below.* Personalize it with the child's name embroidered in silk ribbon. The guardian angel's face is sweetly framed with old-fashioned coiled braids created from black pearl cotton. Spell the child's name again in reverse-appliqué on felt and use the letters as a lampshade trim in your youngster's room.

A child's cozy companion for slumberland, Willie the Whiz is sure to bring sweet dreams—or you can buy them for a nickel!

Better yet, when he's featured in appliqué on the child-size vest, just a wave of Willie's invisible wand will catch a falling star!

"SLEEP IN HEAVENLY PEACE" WALLHANGING

Wallhanging is 32" high x 25" wide, including yo-yos

For information about the materials, tools, techniques, and stitches, read "Tips and Techniques" starting on page 7.

Materials

1 yard of 72"-wide denim wool felt for the backing and banners

❤

1 yard of 72"-wide straw wool felt for the background

❤

One 9" x 12" piece of gold wool felt for the stars

❤

¼ yard each of three cotton prints for the background pieces of the center quilt and the dress appliqués

❤

⅛ yard each of five or more cotton prints in blue, green, burgundy, and tan for the yo-yos, wing appliqués, and pieced border on center quilt

❤

⅛ yard of white or any flesh-color cotton fabric for the face and hand appliqués

❤

⅝ yard of a dark blue cotton print for back of quilt and binding

❤

¼ yard of ⅝"- or ¾"-wide ecru lace

❤

½ yard of low-loft quilt batting or fleece

❤

Black quilting thread and quilting needle

❤

Size 8 DMC pearl cotton: one ball each of black (No. 310), off-white (No. 712)

❤

No. 2 and No. 8 embroidery needles

❤

No. 22 and No. 26 chenille needles

❤

YLI 4mm silk ribbon: one 5-yard reel of yellow gold (No. 54)

❤

YLI 2mm silk ribbon: one 5-yard reel of yellow gold (No. 54)

❤

15 white buttons from ½" to 1⅛" in diameter

❤

Template plastic and permanent-ink marker

❤

Mark-B-Gone marking pens

❤

Prepare Felt Pieces

1. Shrink the wool felt, washing each color separately. Dry in dryer.

2. Fold a large sheet of tracing paper in half. With fold of paper placed on fold line of pattern, trace full-size bottom banner pattern on page 59. Cut out and unfold paper for a complete pattern.

    With fold of paper placed on fold line of pattern, trace small section of top banner pattern on page 59. Matching A to A and B to B trace large section of top banner pattern on page 58. Cut out and unfold for a complete pattern, then finish tracing the words on the second half of the banner.

    Trace each star on pages 59-60 onto tracing paper. Cut out.

3. Trace the corner templates on page 58 onto template plastic. Cut out.

4. From the straw wool felt, cut one 24" x 24" square. Referring to Diagram 1, opposite, trace the curve of each corner template onto corners of the felt square. Cut off the corners.

5. From denim felt, cut one 25" x 31" rectangle. Referring to Diagram 2, opposite, center the straw felt piece ½" below the top 25"-edge of the denim

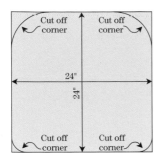

DIAGRAM 1

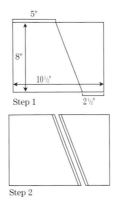

Step 1

Step 2

piece and pin in place. Cut off the top corners of the denim felt, cutting about ½" beyond the edge of the straw felt. Measure and mark the center point of

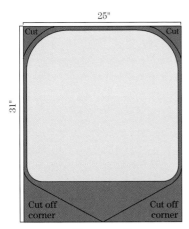

DIAGRAM 2

the bottom edge of the denim piece. Allowing ½" beyond the edges of the bottom corners of the straw felt piece, draw corner lines on the denim felt, meeting at the center point. Cut away the corners.

6. On remaining denim felt, trace around top and bottom banner patterns with Mark-B-Gone marking pen; on gold felt, trace around six star patterns. Cut out.

Transfer the words to top banner. Print your child's name in center of bottom banner. Set aside for later.

Piece Center Quilt

1. Referring to Step 1 in Diagram 3, cut an 8" x 10½" piece of tracing paper. Turn paper so the 8" edges are on the sides. Along the top edge, measure and mark a

spot 5" in from left-hand edge. Along the bottom edge, measure and mark a spot 2½" in from right-hand edge. Draw a diagonal line, connecting the two marks.

Referring to Step 2, cut paper apart along the diagonal line.

2. Choosing two contrasting cotton prints for center of quilt, cut one of each shape just made, adding ¼" seam allowances to the diagonal edges. With the right sides together, sew the two pieces together along the diagonal edges.

3. Trace appliqué patterns on pages 58-60 onto tracing paper or template plastic. Cut out. Referring to the materials list for fabrics and to patterns for numbers, trace around each shape on front of fabric with a disappearing-ink marker. Cut out, adding a ⅛" seam allowance to all edges.

Referring to the photograph on page 42, pin the dress appliqué on the pieced quilt center. Leaving the bottom edge unstitched, slip-stitch the dress in place with matching thread, using the tip of the needle to turn under the ⅛" seam allowance. (Do not press until marker lines have been removed following manufacturer's directions.)

4. From a variety of cotton prints, cut several 3"-wide pieces, varying the length from 1" to 5".

Sew together enough pieces to make a 10½" strip for the top border, a 10½" strip for the right-side border, a 13" strip for the bottom border, and a

13" strip for the left-side border. Press seam allowances to one side.

With right sides together and raw edges matching, sew the 10½" strip to the top of the quilt center; finger-press the seam allowances toward the strip.

5. In the same way, sew the right-side strip in place. Referring to Diagram 4, sew the bottom strip in place, catching the hem of the dress in the seam while stitching the bottom border.

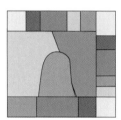

DIAGRAM 4

6. Sew left-hand strip in place. Referring to Diagram 5 and the short dashed lines on the appliqué patterns, arrange the remaining appliqués in place, allowing for the added seam allowances. Pin in place.

Leaving edges that are overlapped unstitched, hand-appliqué the wings in place first. Appliqué the hands next, followed by the sleeves. Add the face last.

DIAGRAM 5

Finish Quilt

1. With off-white pearl cotton, embroider a row of feather stitches along the top edge of the angel's right wing.

With black pearl cotton, embroider a row of feather stitches along the top edge of the angel's left wing.

2. With black pearl cotton, embroider angel's eyes as shown on face pattern.

For her hair, draw two ⅝" circles on each side of face as shown on face pattern. Thread larger needle with three strands of black pearl cotton. Referring to stitch illustration next to face pattern, fill in each circle with a spiral of chain stitches. Outline the top of angel's head between two circles with chain stitches.

3. With matching thread, gather one long edge of lace to fit under angel's face and handstitch in place.

4. With single strands of black and off-white pearl cotton, embroider across the seams of the pieced borders using decorative stitches such as feather stitch, blanket stitch, long and short blanket stitch, and large cross-stitches.

5. From dark blue print, cut a 15" × 17½" piece for back of quilt. From batting, cut a 13" × 15½" piece.

With wrong side up, smooth out backing fabric and center batting on top. Center quilt top, right side up, on top of batting. Baste together.

6. Use black quilting thread to sew a row of quilting stitches on the wing, ¼" inside the feather-stitched edge. Quilt another row ¼" in from first row. Repeat for a total of three or four rows. This is called "echo" quilting.

Echo-quilt the angel's other wing and the visible portions of the center background pieces.

7. On each side edge of quilt, turn ½" of excess backing fabric to the right side and press. Turn remaining ½" to front, covering raw edges of quilt; slip-stitch in place. Turn and slip-stitch the top and bottom edges next.

8. With black quilting thread, quilt borders ¼" in from edge of binding and ¼" in from edge of the center.

Make Yo-Yos

1. For the yo-yo pattern, draw one 3¼"-diameter circle onto template plastic. Cut out.

2. Trace around yo-yo template on wrong side of a variety of cotton prints for a total of 82 yo-yos. Cut out.

3. Thread the hand-sewing needle with matching thread; knot thread ends together. With wrong side of fabric facing up, turn a ⅛" hem to front, hand-sewing it in place with short running stitches. Pull thread to gather circle into a small pouch. Pull thread taut, closing pouch; knot thread, clipping ends close to knot. With gathers centered at top, flatten yo-yo.

Finish Wallhanging

1. Center the quilt on straw felt piece, about 6½" below top edge. Pin in place. Arrange top and bottom banners and pin in place. Remove quilt.

2. With 4mm gold silk ribbon and the larger chenille needle, attach banners with long running stitches.

   Next, use the 4mm silk ribbon to outline-stitch the words on each banner, allowing the letter Y on top banner to fall onto the straw background.

3. Referring to Diagram 2, place straw background onto denim backing. With off-white pearl cotton, blanket-stitch around the edges of straw background.

4. Reposition the quilt in the center of wallhanging. All stitching from this point on is worked through all layers of the fabric and felt.

5. Thread needle with an 18" length of 2mm gold ribbon. Take a stitch just below the center of angel's face, leaving two long tails of ribbon on front of quilt; tie a bow. With 2mm ribbon, attach a small button on top of lace, just below the bow. Stitch another small button just below the first button.

6. Arrange three felt stars on top banner, one on bottom banner, one in angel's hand, and one on background of quilt. Referring to star patterns, place a button in the center of each star and stitch both in place at the same time, using either 4mm or 2mm ribbon, depending on what will pass through holes of button.

7. Arrange six buttons of various sizes on quilt and attach with ribbon.

8. Referring to photo on page 42, arrange a cluster of three yo-yos and one button along the top edge of the quilt. Use silk ribbon to attach the button, while at the same time catching the yo-yos in the stitches.

   In the same way, attach a cluster of two yo-yos and one button to the left-hand side of the bottom banner.

9. Referring to the photo for position, arrange yo-yos all along the denim blue border of the wallhanging, filling in the bottom point. Hand-stitch in place, hiding stitches inside yo-yos.

   Turn over the wallhanging, and carefully trim away any excess denim felt from bottom point.

"ME AND MY PAL" TEDDY BEAR

Finished bear stands about 19" tall.

Note: If this bear is for a child under the age of 3, eliminate the buttons and beads. Instead, sew on the arms and legs without the buttons, and satin-stitch the eyes.

For information about the materials, tools, techniques, and stitches, read "Tips and Techniques" starting on page 7.

Materials

½ yard of 72"-wide straw wool felt for the bear, and moon on hat

♥

One 9" x 12" piece of denim wool felt for the vest

♥

Two 9" x 12" pieces of gold wool felt for the hat and stars on vest

♥

Size 5 DMC pearl cotton: one skein each of black (No. 310), off-white (No. 712), gold (No. 783)

♥

No. 22 or No. 26 chenille needles

♥

Doll needle

♥

YLI 2mm silk ribbon: one 5-yard reel of yellow gold (No. 54)

♥

YLI 32mm silk ribbon: one 5-yard reel of yellow gold (No. 54)

♥

Four ⅞" to 1" two-hole white buttons

♥

Two black 6mm beads for eyes

♥

Polyester stuffing

♥

Mark-B-Gone marking pens

♥

Prepare Pieces

1. Shrink the wool felt, washing each color separately. Dry in dryer.
2. Trace full-size patterns on pages 61-62 onto tracing paper. Cut out.
3. Referring to materials list for suggested colors and to patterns for numbers, trace around patterns on felt. Cut out.

Teddy Bear

1. All patterns include a ¼" seam allowance where needed. All stitching is done with right sides together.
2. With matching thread, machine-sew the two body pieces together, leaving an opening in back for turning. Turn right side out and firmly stuff. Turn in raw edges and hand-sew closed.
3. Machine-sew two head pieces together, leaving the bottom edge open. Turn right side out and firmly stuff. Turn under raw edges and slip head over top of body. Hand-stitch head in place.
4. Referring to broken line of snout on head pattern and to Diagram 1, push snout upward so line meets head as shown; hand-stitch in place along each side of face.

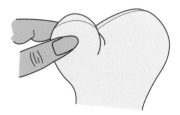

DIAGRAM 1

5. Machine-sew two sets of ears together along large curved edges, leaving bottom ends open for turning. Turn right side out and lightly stuff. Turn under raw edges and hand-sew closed, gathering the edge slightly so ears curve. Position on head along curved line and hand-sew ears in place.

6. Referring to Diagram 2, satin-stitch nose with black pearl cotton. Add bead eyes.

Satin stitch

DIAGRAM 2

7. Machine-sew two sets of arms and two sets of legs together, leaving openings in back for turning. Turn right side out and firmly stuff. Turn in raw edges and hand-sew closed.

8. Thread doll needle with a long length of off-white pearl cotton. Referring to pattern for position, place a button on bear's shoulder; insert needle through button and through bear's arm; then through bear's body to opposite side and through remaining arm and second button. Remove needle, leaving long tails on each side of buttons.

   Repeat the last step, pulling a second length of pearl cotton through remaining holes of two buttons. On one side of the bear, tie the ends together. On the opposite side of bear, tie the ends together, pulling thread just taut enough so limbs move but do not hang loose. Make a double knot and trim off excess pearl cotton, leaving tails about ¼" to ½" long. Add legs in the same way.

Collar

1. Machine-sew short ends of wide silk ribbon together, forming a loop. The seam will be positioned at center back.

2. Thread smaller chenille needle with 1 yard of 2mm silk ribbon. Beginning at center front, sew a gathering stitch along one long edge of wide ribbon. Remove needle and slip ribbon collar over teddy's head. Pull gathering thread to fit the neck and tie a bow.

Vest

1. With matching thread, machine-sew two front vest pieces to back vest piece at shoulders and side seams. Turn right side out.

2. Fold back two front vest pieces along the fold lines as marked on front pattern, and pin in place. Referring to Diagram 3, use gold pearl cotton to sew running stitches along the vest's edges.

3. Referring to Diagram 3, arrange and pin the stars on vest. With gold pearl cotton, attach each star with a single French knot in the center of the star. Dress teddy.

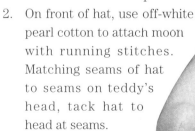

DIAGRAM 3

Hat

1. Machine-sew two hat pieces together, starting and stopping stitching at the cuff fold line. Leave cuff end open. Turn hat right side out and turn up cuff along fold lines. Use gold pearl cotton and a running stitch to hold cuff in place.

2. On front of hat, use off-white pearl cotton to attach moon with running stitches. Matching seams of hat to seams on teddy's head, tack hat to head at seams.

"ME AND MY PAL" VEST
Vest shown is size 4

Note: The recommended vest pattern is multi-sized. If another commercial vest pattern is substituted, purchase extra wool felt. If necessary, reduce or enlarge the appliqué patterns on a copy machine to fit your vest.

For information about the materials, tools, techniques, and stitches, read "Tips and Techniques" starting on page 7.

Materials
Indigo Junction's "It's a Small World" multi-size vest pattern (No. IJ447)

¾ yard of 72"-wide denim wool felt for the vest, plus teddy's vest and pocket pieces

One 9" x 12" piece of gold wool felt for the hats and stars

Two 9" x 12" pieces of straw wool felt for the bear and moons

Size 5 DMC pearl cotton: one skein each of black (No. 310), off-white (No. 712), gold (No. 783)

No. 20 and No. 22 chenille needles

½ yard of gold-nugget color Offray 2mm chainette

Two ¾" white buttons

Two star-shape brass charms

Mark-B-Gone marking pens: white ink and disappearing-ink

Prepare Pieces
1. Shrink the wool felt, washing each color separately. Dry in dryer.
2. From commercial vest pattern, trace and cut out vest back and vest front pieces, omitting any lining or facing pieces that may come with pattern.
3. Referring to Diagram 1, use the white marker to trace around the vest front pattern, reversed vest front pattern, and vest back pattern on front of denim felt. Do not yet cut out.

DIAGRAM 1   DIAGRAM 2

4. Referring to diagrams on page 65, trace individual appliqué patterns. Cut out.
5. Referring to materials list for suggested colors and to diagrams for numbers, trace around patterns on felt; cut out.

Right Front Vest
1. Referring to Diagram 1, place the body piece on the right front vest area. Referring to the patterns for position, place the vest on the body and an arm on top. Slip the remaining arm under the body, off-setting it as shown on pattern and diagram. Pin in place. Referring to black dashed lines on body pattern, position one leg on top of body and one underneath body. Off-set the bottom leg as seen in diagram. Pin in place.
2. With gold pearl cotton and running stitches, sew the vest in place.

3. With off-white pearl cotton, blanket-stitch all exposed edges of teddy's body.

4. With off-white pearl cotton and running stitches, attach small moon to teddy's hat. Referring to black dashed line on teddy's head for position, pin the hat in place. Use gold pearl cotton and running stitches to attach hat.

5. With off-white pearl cotton, blanket-stitch two ears together around the large curved edge; then, blanket-stitch the remaining edge to teddy's head.

6. With gold pearl cotton, blanket-stitch around teddy's vest so each stitch reaches the previously made running stitches. Pin pocket on teddy's vest and attach with gold running stitches, continuing the stitches across top of pocket without attaching it to vest. Referring to pattern for position, add two gold French knots. At each French knot, sew one star-shape charm.

7. Referring to Diagram 3, embroider nose with several black satin stitches and a few outline stitches. With black pearl cotton, add a French knot eye.

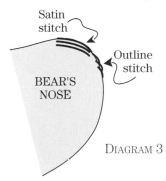

Satin stitch

Outline stitch

BEAR'S NOSE

DIAGRAM 3

8. Referring to patterns for position, use gold pearl cotton to attach buttons.

9. Fold chainette in half and wrap folded end around top point of lassoed star. Pin star in place, and attach with gold pearl cotton and a running stitch. Below star tie two ends of chainette together with an overhand knot. Tie again about 1½" to 2" below first knot. Thread ends of chainette onto No. 20 needle and pull

between hands so bear appears to be holding the ends.

Left Front Vest

1. Referring to Diagram 2, arrange and pin felt pieces on left front vest area.

2. With off-white pearl cotton and running stitches, attach the moon. Embroider the eye with black pearl cotton.

3. With gold pearl cotton, blanket-stitch the straight edge of the hat to the moon, attach the remaining edges with running stitches, and attach three stars with running stitches.

Finish Vest

1. Cut out vest pieces on white lines. With right sides together, machine-sew two front pieces to the back vest piece at shoulders and side seams; turn.

2. To finish, turn under seam allowance around armholes and outer edges of vest as you hand-stitch them in place with gold pearl cotton and long running stitches.

LAMP SHADE TRIM

Each letter is about 3½" high x 3" wide with yo-yos

For information about the materials, tools, techniques, and stitches, read "Tips and Techniques" starting on page 7.

Materials

One 9" x 12" piece of denim wool felt for two top circles and two backing circles

One 9" x 12" piece of straw wool felt for two top circles and two backing circles

⅛ yard each or scraps of four coordinating cotton prints for center circles and yo-yos

Matching threads and hand-sewing needle

Size 5 DMC pearl cotton: one skein each of blue (No. 825), off-white (No. 712)

No. 2 crewel embroidery needle

Four white two-hole buttons varying in size from ½" to ¾"

YLI 2mm silk ribbon: one 5-yard reel of blue (No. 45), one 5-yard reel of off-white (No. 156)

Mark-B-Gone marking pens

Prepare Pieces

1. From full-size patterns opposite, trace four top circles, and the inside pieces for two letters *B* and one letter *A* onto tracing paper. Trace a letter in the center of each top circle, spelling out the word *BABY*. Cut out.

2. Referring to materials list for suggested colors and to diagrams for numbers, trace around the patterns on felt. Cut out. Use embroidery scissors to cut out the letters from top circles.

3. For the yo-yo pattern, draw a 2½"-diameter circle on paper. Cut out. Trace the center circle and backing circle patterns. Cut out. On the wrong side of each cotton print, trace around the center circle pattern and the yo-yo pattern once. Cut out.

4. Trace around backing circle pattern twice on front of denim felt, and twice on front of straw felt. Do not cut out.

Stitch Design

1. Place each center circle in the center of a traced backing circle. Pin a top circle on top of a center circle with the fabric showing through cutouts.

2. Using either white or blue pearl cotton, sew running stitches around each letter. Use running stitches to add the inside pieces to the letters *A* and *B*.

3. With contrasting color pearl cotton, blanket-stitch each top circle to the backing circle. Cut out backing circles.

Finish Sign

1. Referring to "Make Yo-Yos" on page 47, make four yo-yos.

2. Center one button on top of gathered side of each yo-yo. Tie button in place. Tack one yo-yo to top of each letter.

3. For each ornament, cut a 30" piece of either the blue or the off-white silk ribbon. Fold one length in half. While holding the two loose ends in one hand, hook the fold around a finger on the opposite hand and rotate that finger to twist the ribbon. Continue twisting until the ribbon begins to feel stiff; then, carefully fold this length in half, holding both ends in one hand and letting go of the new fold so the ribbon twists onto itself. Tie loose ends and hand-stitch to back of letter.

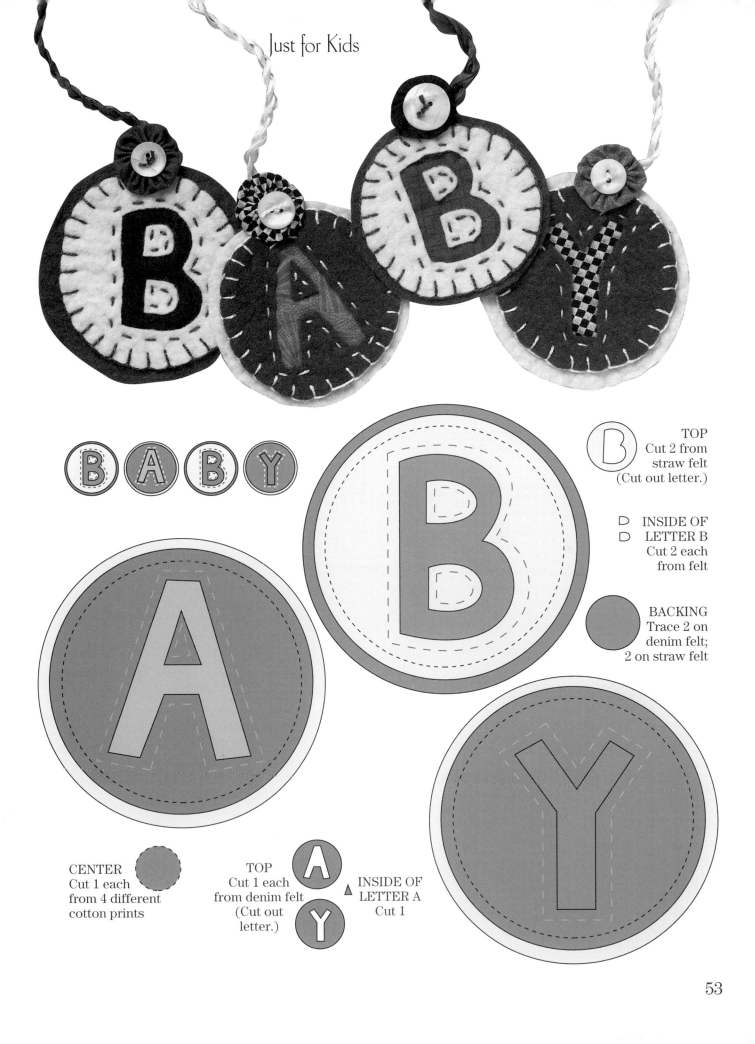

TOP
Cut 2 from
straw felt
(Cut out letter.)

INSIDE OF
LETTER B
Cut 2 each
from felt

BACKING
Trace 2 on
denim felt;
2 on straw felt

CENTER
Cut 1 each
from 4 different
cotton prints

TOP
Cut 1 each
from denim felt
(Cut out
letter.)

INSIDE OF
LETTER A
Cut 1

MOON AND STARS PINS
Each pin is 2½" high x 2½" wide

For information about the materials, tools, techniques, and stitches, read "Tips and Techniques" starting on page 7.

Materials
FOR DESIGN NO. 1:
One 9" x 12" piece or scraps of denim wool felt for the front and back squares

Three ⁷⁄₁₆" four-hole white shirt buttons

DMC six-strand embroidery floss: blue (No. 825), brown (No. 801), gold (No. 782)

FOR DESIGN NO. 2:
One 9" x 12" piece or scraps of burgundy wool felt for the front and back squares

One 9" x 12" piece or scrap of champagne wool felt for the moon

One ⁵⁄₁₆" four-hole white shirt button

DMC six-strand embroidery floss: black (No. 310), gold (No. 782)

FOR EACH DESIGN:
Embroidery needle

One 2⅛" square of gold cotton print for center square

One 1" pin-back

Mark-B-Gone marking pens

Prepare Pieces
1. Referring to diagrams opposite, trace individual pieces. Cut out.
2. Referring to materials list for suggested colors and to diagrams for numbers, trace around the patterns on felt. Cut out. Use embroidery scissors to cut the moon or star shape out of the front felt piece.

Stitch Design No. 1
1. Center the fabric square, right side up, on top of the back felt square. Pin the front felt square, right side up, on top of the fabric square.
2. Separate six-strand floss and use single strands for all stitching. Referring to pattern, use gold floss and a running stitch to sew around moon cutout about ⅛" outside cut edge.
3. Referring to pattern, use blue floss and running stitches to sew moon shape about ⅛" inside cut edge.
4. With brown floss and straight stitches, embroider eyelashes.
5. Referring to pattern, use gold floss to double blanket-stitch together the edges of front and back squares.
6. Attach buttons as shown on pattern.

I've always loved the dimensional effect of appliqué, but reverse appliqué provides an unusual contrast that works particularly well with felt.

Stitch Design No. 2

1. Separate six-strand floss, using single strands for all stitching except black eyelashes. Referring to pattern for position, use gold floss and long straight stitches to attach the cheek.

2. With three strands of black floss and straight stitches, embroider eyelashes. (A single strand of black No. 8 or No. 5 pearl cotton can be substituted.)

3. Blanket-stitch moon to front felt piece with a regular or double blanket-stitch.

4. Center fabric square, right side up, on top of back felt square. Pin front felt square, right side up, on top of fabric square.

5. Referring to pattern, use gold floss and running stitches to sew around star cutout about ⅛" outside the cut edge.

6. Referring to pattern, use gold floss to blanket-stitch the edges of the front and back squares together, using the same technique described for moon.

7. Attach button as shown on pattern.

Finish Pin

1. Being careful not to sew through front of design, hand-sew pin-back in place. Either center the pin-back about 1" below the top edge of the pin or turn the pin diagonally and center the pin about 1" below the top point.

DESIGN NO. 1

BACK
Cut 1
from felt

CENTER
Cut 1 from
cotton print

FRONT
Cut 1
from felt
(Cut out
moon.)

DESIGN NO. 2

BACK
Cut 1
from felt

CENTER
Cut 1 from
cotton print

FRONT
Cut 1
from felt
(Cut out
star.)

CHEEK
Cut 1

MOON
Cut 1

"SWEET DREAMS" SIGN

Sign is 8" high x 9½" wide with yo-yos

For information about the materials, tools, techniques, and stitches, read "Tips and Techniques" starting on page 7.

Materials

One 9" x 12" piece of denim wool felt for the front piece

❤

One 9" x 12" piece of straw wool felt for the back piece

❤

One 9" x 12" piece of gold wool felt for the stars

❤

Scraps of several cotton prints for yo-yos

❤

YLI 2mm silk ribbon: one 5-yard reel of yellow gold (No. 54)

❤

No. 8 crewel embroidery or No. 26 chenille needle

❤

Four white two-hole buttons from ⅜" to ¾" in diameter

❤

½ yard of burgundy drapery cord

❤

One 4" x 8½" piece of cardboard

❤

Mark-B-Gone marking pens

❤

Prepare Pieces

1. From full-size patterns opposite, trace one back piece, one front piece, and each star onto tracing paper. For the yo-yo pattern, draw a 3¼"-diameter circle on paper. Cut out.
2. Referring to materials list for suggested colors and to diagrams for numbers, trace around patterns on felt; cut out stars. Leave front and back pieces uncut.
3. Referring to manufacturer's directions, use transfer pen or pencil to transfer lettering to front piece.

Stitch Design

1. Before cutting out the front piece, embroider the sign with silk ribbon and outline stitch. Cut out front piece.
2. Arrange and pin stars on front piece. Position a button in the center of each star and embroider in place with silk ribbon as shown on pattern.
3. Center the front piece on the uncut back piece. Center the cardboard in between and stitch front piece in place using silk ribbon and a running stitch, stitching just outside the edge of cardboard. Cut out the back piece.

Finish Sign

1. Referring to "Make Yo-Yos" on page 47, make 10 yo-yos.
2. Referring to the photograph below for position, arrange yo-yos along bottom edge of sign. Tack in place.
3. Tie a knot in each end of drapery cord. Tack each knot to a back corner of the sign.

BACK
Trace 1
onto felt

Sweet Dreams
5¢

FRONT
Transfer 1 onto felt

STARS
Cut 1 each

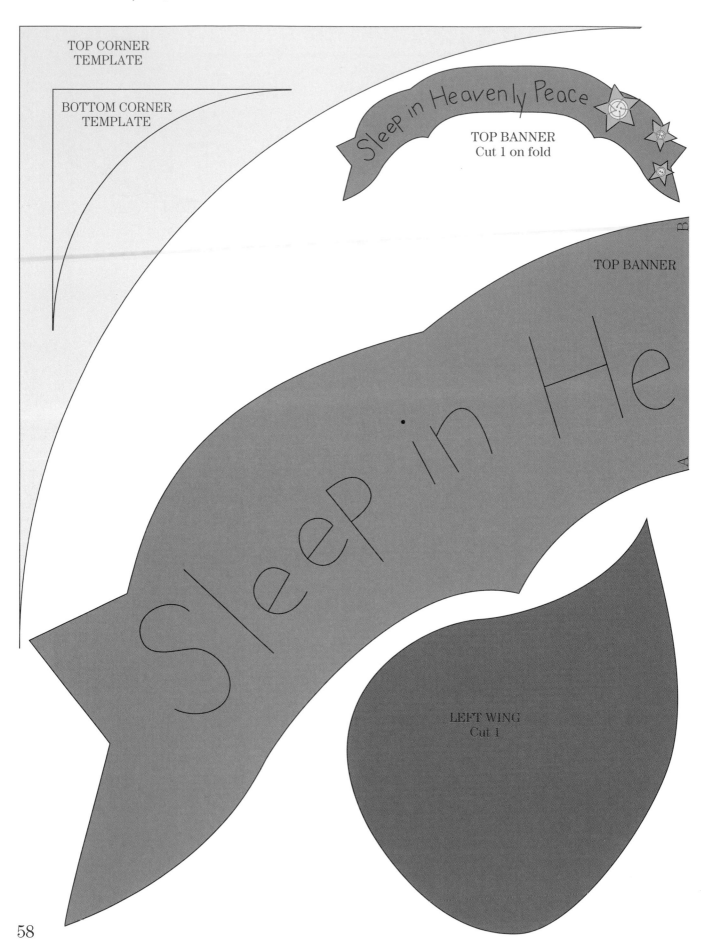

TOP CORNER
TEMPLATE

BOTTOM CORNER
TEMPLATE

Sleep in Heavenly Peace

TOP BANNER
Cut 1 on fold

TOP BANNER

Sleep in He

Sleep in

LEFT WING
Cut 1

TOP BANNER

Place on fold

avenly Peace

STARS
Cut 1 each

BOTTOM BANNER

Place on fold

BOTTOM BANNER
Cut 1 on fold

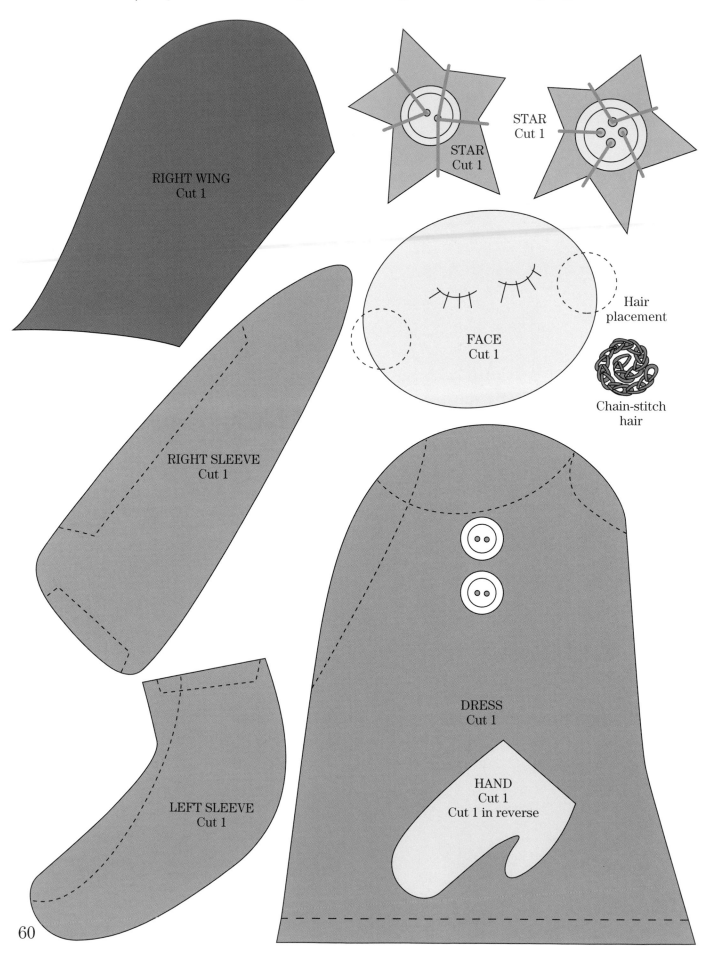

RIGHT WING
Cut 1

STAR
Cut 1

STAR
Cut 1

STAR
Cut 1

Hair
placement

FACE
Cut 1

Chain-stitch
hair

RIGHT SLEEVE
Cut 1

DRESS
Cut 1

LEFT SLEEVE
Cut 1

HAND
Cut 1
Cut 1 in reverse

60

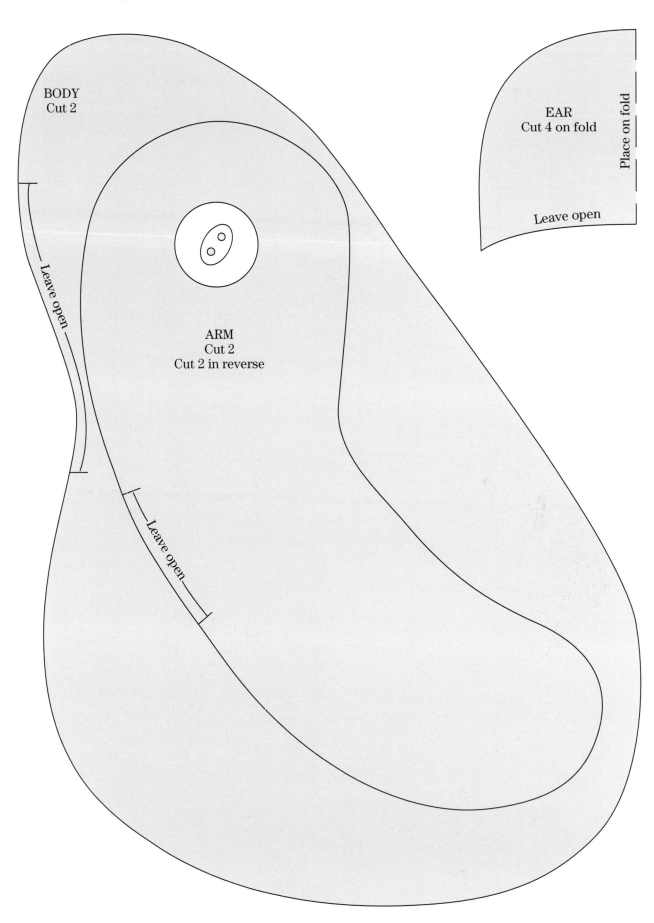

BODY
Cut 2

Leave open

ARM
Cut 2
Cut 2 in reverse

Leave open

EAR
Cut 4 on fold

Place on fold

Leave open

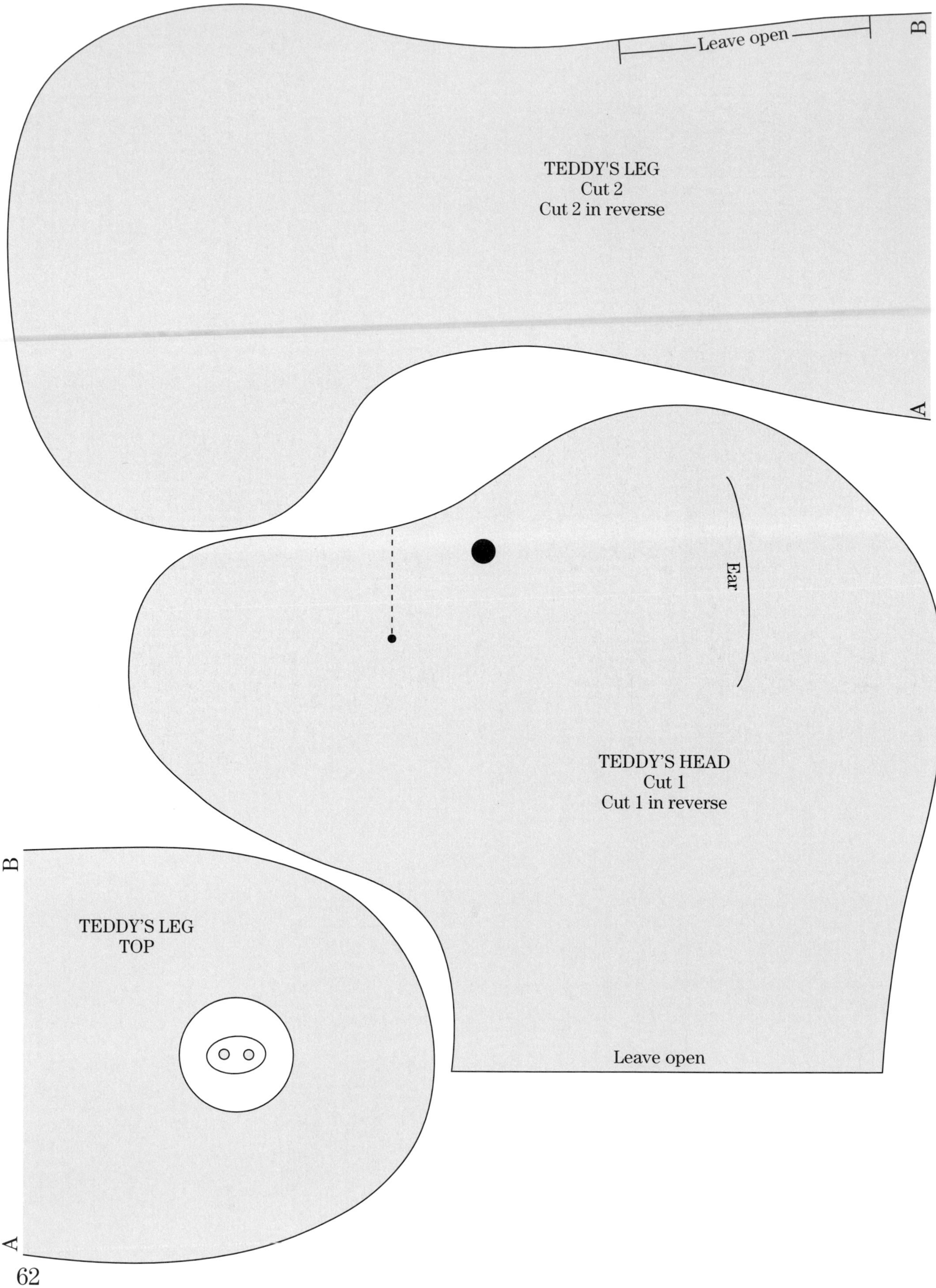

B

Leave open

TEDDY'S LEG
Cut 2
Cut 2 in reverse

A

Ear

TEDDY'S HEAD
Cut 1
Cut 1 in reverse

B

TEDDY'S LEG
TOP

Leave open

A

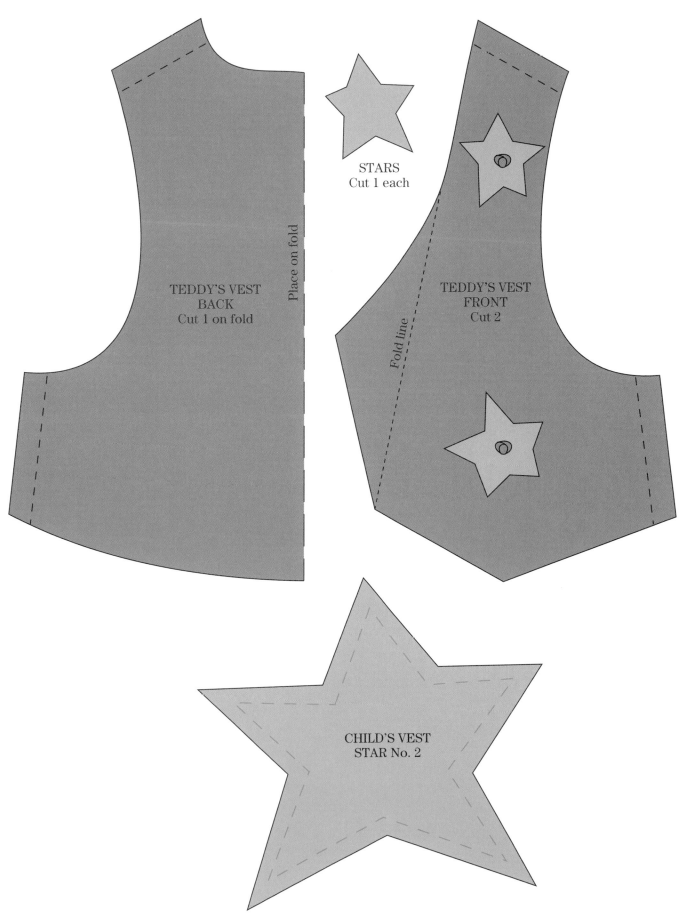

STARS
Cut 1 each

Place on fold

TEDDY'S VEST
BACK
Cut 1 on fold

Fold line

TEDDY'S VEST
FRONT
Cut 2

CHILD'S VEST
STAR No. 2

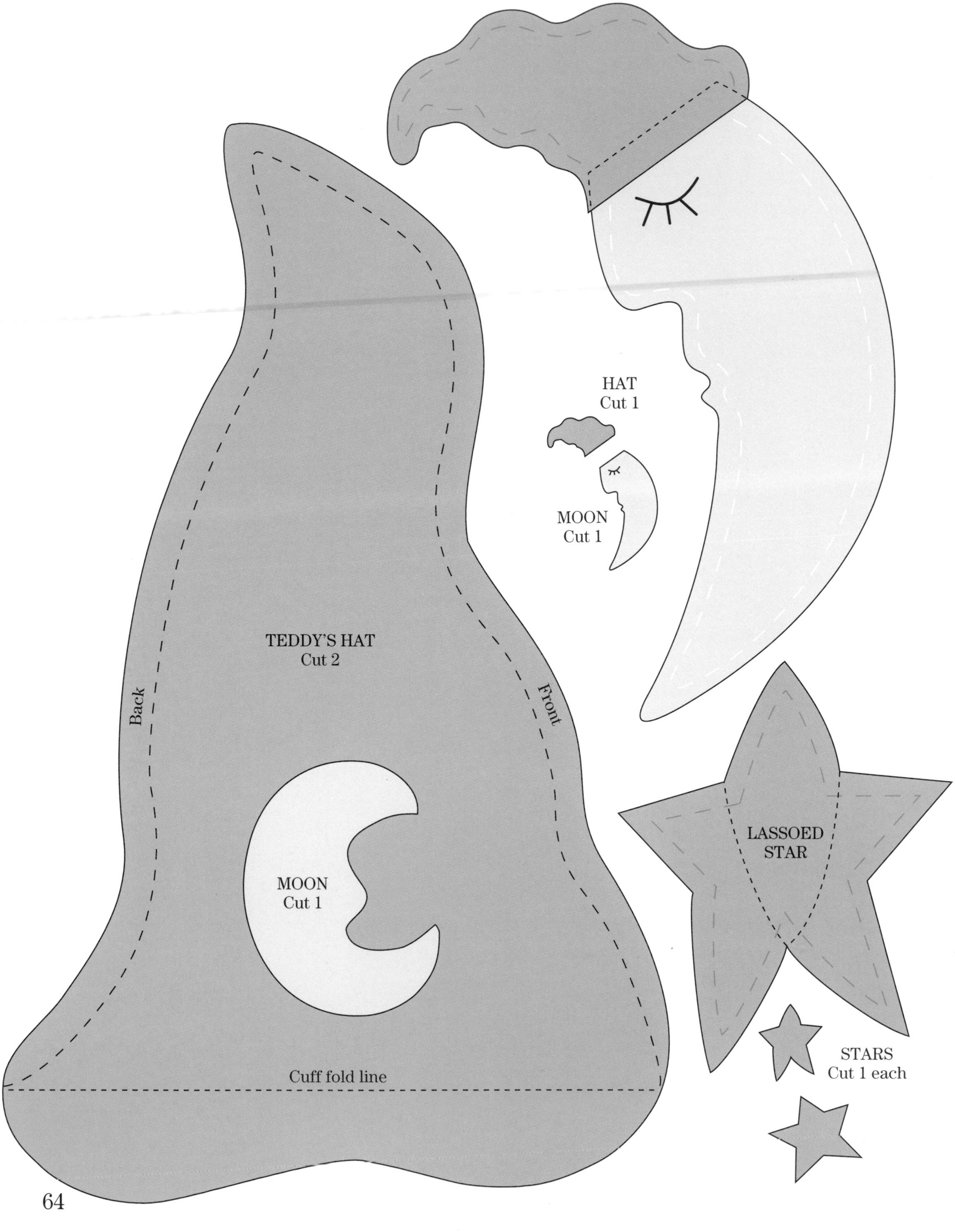

HAT
Cut 1

MOON
Cut 1

TEDDY'S HAT
Cut 2

Back

Front

MOON
Cut 1

Cuff fold line

LASSOED
STAR

STARS
Cut 1 each

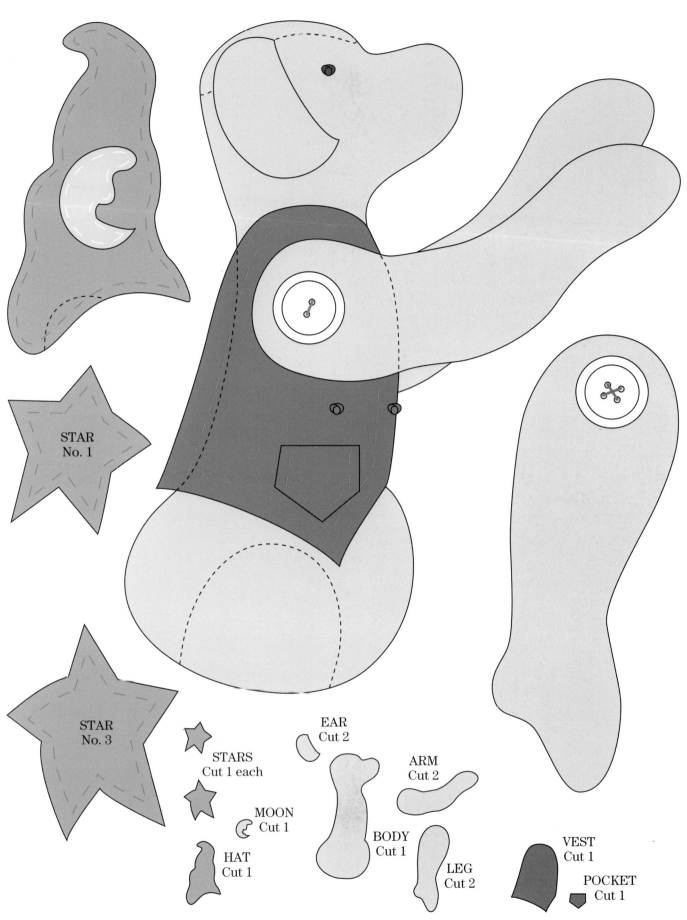

STAR
No. 1

STAR
No. 3

EAR
Cut 2

STARS
Cut 1 each

ARM
Cut 2

MOON
Cut 1

BODY
Cut 1

HAT
Cut 1

LEG
Cut 2

VEST
Cut 1

POCKET
Cut 1

Harvest Home

Bring home nature's beauty in a collection of decorative accents ablaze with the deep, rich colors of autumn leaves. For the felt wallhanging, below, start with a touch of whimsy—a charming angel kitty complete with architectural wings—and then add the bird, birdhouse, and a scattering of leaves.

To achieve a mottled effect reminiscent of primitive hand-dyed fabrics, simply over-dye the wool felt before you cut out the pattern pieces.

Complement the wallhanging with a leaf-embellished table runner trimmed with a traditional pen-wiper border. (Pen-wipers were tongue-shape pieces of flannel or felt intended for wiping the excess ink from steel pens.)

Plan ahead, and over-dye enough felt to make the leaves in multiples in shades of autumn.

Use the faux fall foliage for a quick and easy final touch—on the stem of a water goblet, the handle of a rustic basket, the base of a candlestick; or in a matter of minutes you can create a napkin ring by adding a cluster of leaves to a rustic mini-grapevine wreath.

ANGEL KITTY WALLHANGING

Wallhanging is 30" wide x 36" long

Note: More than 40 leaves can be cut from the materials listed. Leftover leaves can be used for other projects in this chapter, or they can be added to a centerpiece, tied to a basket, or attached to a wreath.

For information about materials, tools, techniques, and stitches, read "Tips and Techniques" starting on page 7.

Materials

1 yard of 72"-wide black wool felt for the background and tongues

♥

⅜ yard of 72"-wide straw wool felt for the dyed leaves, dress, and sleeves

♥

⅜ yard of 72"-wide silver gray wool felt for the wings, lattice pieces, birdhouse stand, post, roof, and heart

♥

One 9" x 12" piece of camel wool felt for the face, paws, and feet

♥

One 9" x 12" piece of denim wool felt for the bird

♥

One 9" x 12" piece of red wool felt for the leaves and birdhouse

♥

One 9" x 12" piece of copper wool felt for the leaves

♥

Dritz cold-water dyes:
Koala Brown, Leaf Green, Tartan Green, Nasturtium, Sahara Sun

♥

Five 1-quart glass canning jars

♥

Rubber bands

♥

Coffee to dye dress

♥

Size 5 DMC pearl cotton: one ball or two skeins of black (No. 310), one skein of dark beige (No. 642)

♥

Size 8 DMC pearl cotton: one ball each of light beige (No. 822), variegated gray

♥

No. 20 and No. 22 chenille needle

♥

3 yards of gold-nugget color Offray 2mm chainette

♥

6" piece of 1¼"-wide ecru lace trim

♥

Three white ⅜" buttons for dress

♥

13 autumn-color buttons varying in size from ½" to ⅝" for tongues

♥

Tulip Pearl Dimensional Paint: Liquid Pearl, Silver, Snow White

♥

Tulip paint extender

♥

Flat artist's brush: ¼" to ½" wide with stiff bristles

♥

Black fine-line permanent-ink marker

♥

Template plastic

♥

Mark-B-Gone marking pens: white ink and disappearing-ink

♥

Prepare Fabrics

1. Shrink the wool felt, washing each color separately. Dry in dryer.
2. Following package directions, mix a different color dye in each of five jars, using a third of each package per jar. From straw felt cut four 9" x 12" pieces.

   Scrunch up the red felt piece and each of the four straw felt pieces into a separate ball, wrapping them with rubber bands so one ball fits inside each canning jar. Put the red ball into the Koala Brown dye. Put a straw ball into

My one-of-a-kind folk art animal dolls inspired me to combine a hand-painted feline face with over-dyed wool felt. The result is an angel kitty with whimsical accents such as architectural wings and a birdhouse!

each of the remaining four colors. Remove after 45 minutes to 1 hour. Unwrap to check color. The colors should be uneven, like autumn leaves, but if any portion of the dyed piece appears too light, re-scrunch and wrap the felt, and place it back into the dye. Check again after 30 minutes. Dry in a dryer. Use copper felt undyed.

3. For the dress, dip the remaining straw felt in strong coffee. Dry in a dryer.

Prepare Pieces

1. Trace the full-size leaf patterns on pages 74-75 and full-size tongue pattern on page 75 onto template plastic. Cut out.

2. Referring to the diagrams and the remaining full-size patterns on pages 76-79, trace individual pieces onto tracing paper, matching A to A and B to B or C to C and D to D to complete larger pieces. Cut out.

3. With white or disappearing-ink marker, trace around the leaf patterns on the copper and dyed felts, varying the shapes and colors for a total of 23 leaves. Cut out. Use disappearing-ink marker to draw veins freehand.

4. Referring to materials list for suggested colors and to diagrams for numbers, use disappearing-ink marker to trace around tracing paper patterns on felt. Cut out.

   Use embroidery scissors to cut out the inside detail areas on the wings, birdhouse stand, corner lattice pieces, and lattice point.

5. Set aside one set of cat's paws, feet, and head. Mix paint extender with Liquid Pearl Dimensional Paint and use to paint top surfaces of remaining set. Let dry.

   Using the paint writer tip on the dimensional paint bottles, add Silver nose and stripes on cat's head. Let dry. Add Snow White stripes between Silver stripes. Let dry. With black permanent-ink marker, draw eyes and eyelashes, allowing some white to show through on eyes. Mark dots for position of whiskers. The white dashed lines on pattern are stitching lines.

6. Referring to Diagram 1, use a white marking pen to draw a 30"-wide x 33"-high rectangle on a large piece of pre-shrunk black wool. Measure and mark bottom corners as shown in diagram. Cut out, leaving an extra 1" or 2" of fabric all around.
   Note: On large projects, felt edges may stretch out of shape while appliqués are being stitched in place. The extra fabric is allowed so any over-stretched edges can be trimmed off.

7. With white marking pen, trace around tongue template 13 times on remaining black felt. Cut out.

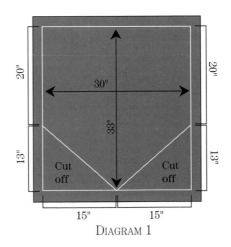

DIAGRAM 1

Begin Stitching Design

1. Pin the wing piece in place, centering it about 10" below the top white line. Use long-and-short blanket stitches and variegated gray pearl cotton thread to stitch in place.

2. Referring to the full-size patterns and Diagram 2 for position, arrange the birdhouse on top of the wing. The bottom of the post should butt up against the top edge of the wing 2¼" to 2½" in from the left-hand edge of the wing; pin in place.

3. Use variegated gray pearl cotton and running stitches to attach the post and the birdhouse. Use variegated gray to blanket-stitch the birdhouse-stand pieces and the heart in place. Use running stitches to attach the straight edges of the roof, and blanket stitches to attach the scalloped edges.

4. Referring to the full-size patterns and Diagram 2 for position, arrange bird about 3½" above the wing on right-hand side of wallhanging. Pin in place.

5. Use variegated gray pearl cotton to blanket-stitch the tail feather end of bird's body. Use running stitches to attach the rest of body and two wings. Attach the beak with running stitches along the edge that joins head, letting the front of the beak hang loose. Use beige pearl cotton to embroider eye with three short straight stitches as seen on pattern.

Stitch Angel Kitty

1. Place each painted paw, foot, and face on top of its matching unpainted felt piece. With the light beige pearl cotton, blanket-stitch around all the edges. Referring to the white dashed lines on face pattern, use light beige pearl cotton and running stitches to outline bottom of each ear.

2. Referring to photo on page 66 and to Diagram 2 for help with placement, arrange cat's dress on wallhanging. Leaving bottom edge unstitched for now, use light beige pearl cotton and running stitches to attach dress.

3. Referring to pattern for placement, arrange sleeves and paws on dress. Use light beige pearl cotton and running stitches to attach sleeves, catching the wrist of each paw in the stitches. Let paws hang loose.

DIAGRAM 2

4. Thread No. 20 needle with a 9" length of chainette. Referring to pattern for placement of bows on sleeves, take a small stitch in the center of one wrist. Remove needle, leaving two long ends of chainette on front of sleeve. Tie ends together and make a bow. Trim ends as needed. Repeat on remaining sleeve.

5. Referring to short dashed lines on patterns for placement, slip feet under bottom of dress. Thread No. 20 needle with a 15" length of chainette. Referring to gold dashed lines on pattern, use long running stitches to attach bottom of dress to wallhanging, while at the same time catching feet in the stitches. Let feet hang loose.

6. Referring to patterns for placement, use light beige pearl cotton to add a large cross-stitch at the bend of each elbow and a row of cross-stitches across the bottom of the dress.

7. Referring to short dashed line at top of dress pattern, position cat's head on dress. Thread No. 20 chenille needle with dark beige pearl cotton and make a knot about 2" to 3" from the end. Insert needle through a whisker dot, pulling it all the way through to the back of the wallhanging, then bring needle back to the front at another dot. Cut thread, leaving a 2" to 3" tail, and tie a knot close to cat's face. Continuing in this way, add remaining whiskers. Trim length of whiskers as desired.

8. With chainette, sew a running stitch along the top long edge of the lace, leaving two long tails in the center for a bow. Pull gathers to fit neckline and tie bow. Hand-stitch gathered edge of lace to neckline.

9. Referring to dress pattern for position, use light beige pearl cotton thread to attach buttons.

Finish Wallhanging

1. With a 30" length of black pearl cotton, blanket-stitch around curved edge of one tongue, leaving the straight end unstitched; repeat for all tongues.

2. Cut black background fabric on white lines. Referring to Diagram 2, arrange tongues along bottom of wallhanging. Pin tongues in place, underlapping the wallhanging ½". Pin lattice point in place.

3. With black pearl cotton, blanket-stitch the angled edges of the wallhanging, while at the same time attaching the tongues and the lattice point. Finish attaching lattice point with variegated gray pearl cotton and long-and-short blanket stitches.

4. Pin the corner lattice pieces in place. With black pearl cotton, blanket-stitch remaining edges of wallhanging, while at the same time attaching the corner lattice pieces.

   Finish attaching corner lattice pieces with variegated gray pearl cotton and long-and-short blanket stitches.

5. With black pearl cotton, embroider veins on each leaf. For the center vein, use a long straight stitch then, while holding it in place along the curve, add two or three tiny couching stitches. Use shorter straight stitches for remaining veins, holding each curve in place with a single couching stitch in the center of the vein.

6. Referring to the photo on page 66 for placement, arrange 23 leaves on the wallhanging. Allow some portions of leaves to fall off onto tongues and make certain to place one leaf under cat's paws. Pin in place.

7. Using running stitches and black pearl cotton, attach leaves, stitching ⅛" inside edges. On those portions of leaves that fall onto tongues, sew the running stitch through the leaf only. Do not stitch the leaves to the tongues.

8. Alternating the colors, sew one button to each tongue.

9. Thread No. 20 chenille needle with a 32" length of chainette. Sew through top of leaf in cat's paws. Take another stitch just under bird's beak. Remove needle.

   Thread needle with opposite end of chainette and pull this end through the back of one of the cat's paw. Remove needle and arrange chainette so it drapes between each of these points in a pleasing way. Cut off any excess on either end. Knot the ends.

AUTUMN LEAVES TABLE RUNNER

Runner is 15" wide x 38½" long

Note: More than 40 leaves can be cut from the materials listed. Leftover leaves can be used for other projects in this chapter.

For information about materials, tools, techniques, and stitches, read "Tips and Techniques" starting on page 7.

Materials

⅝ yard of 72"-wide black wool felt for the runner and tongues

♥

One 9" x 12" piece of red wool felt for the leaves

♥

One 9" x 12" piece of copper wool felt for the leaves

♥

Four 9" x 12" pieces of straw wool felt for dyed leaves

♥

Dritz cold-water dyes:
Koala Brown, Leaf Green, Tartan Green, Nasturtium, Sahara Sun

♥

Five 1-quart glass canning jars

♥

Rubber bands

♥

Size 5 DMC pearl cotton: one ball or two skeins of black (No. 310)

♥

No. 2 crewel embroidery needle

♥

1½ yards of black ⅜" cotton cording with lip by Hollywood Trim

♥

18 fall-color buttons varying ½" to ⅝" in sizes

♥

Template plastic and permanent-ink marker

♥

Mark-B-Gone marking pens: white ink and disappearing-ink

♥

Prepare Pieces

1. Shrink the wool felt, washing each color separately. Dry in dryer.
2. Following package directions, mix a different color dye in each of five jars, using a third of each package per jar.

   Scrunch up the red felt piece and each straw felt piece into a separate ball, wrapping each with rubber bands so one ball fits inside each canning jar. Put the red ball into the Koala Brown dye. Put a straw ball into each of the remaining four jars. Remove after 45 minutes to 1 hour. Unwrap to check color. The colors should be uneven, like autumn leaves, but if any portion of the dyed piece appears too light, re-scrunch and wrap the felt, placing it back into the dye. Check again after 30 minutes. Dry in a dryer. Use copper felt undyed.
3. Trace full-size leaf patterns on pages 74–75 and full-size tongue pattern on page 75 onto template plastic. Cut out.
4. With white or disappearing-ink marker, trace around leaf patterns on copper and dyed felts, varying the shapes and colors for a total of 32 leaves. Cut out. Use the disappearing-ink marker to draw the veins freehand.
5. From pre-shrunk black wool felt, cut one 14" x 34" rectangle.

Use white marking pen to mark the ends as shown in Diagram 1. Cut off the corners.

6. On remaining black felt, trace around tongue template 18 times. Cut out.

Stitch Design

1. With a 20" length of black pearl cotton, blanket-stitch around the curved edge of each tongue, leaving the straight end unstitched.
2. Referring to Diagram 2, arrange nine tongues along each end of runner. Pin tongues in place overlapping runner ⅜".
3. With black pearl cotton, blanket-stitch the angled edges of the table runner, attaching the tongues as you stitch.
4. Cut cotton cording into two 26" lengths. With the lip placed under the table runner, and the felt edge of the runner butted up against the cording, pin the cording to each long edge, hiding ends

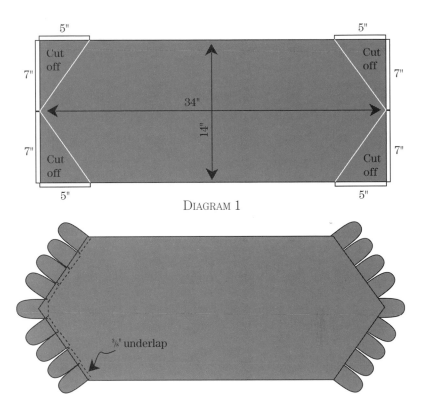

DIAGRAM 1

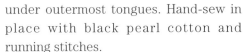

DIAGRAM 2

under outermost tongues. Hand-sew in place with black pearl cotton and running stitches.

5. With black pearl cotton, embroider veins on each leaf. For the center vein, use a long straight stitch, then while holding it in place along the curve add two or three tiny couching stitches. Use shorter straight stitches for remaining veins, holding each curve in place with a single couching stitch in the center of the vein.

Finish Runner

1. Arrange 32 leaves around table runner. At each end, allow portions of leaves to fall off onto tongues. Pin in place.
2. Using running stitches and black pearl cotton, attach leaves, stitching about ⅛" inside edges. On those portions of leaves that fall onto tongues, sew the running stitches through the leaf only.
3. Alternating the colors, sew one button to each tongue.

FAUX FALL FOLIAGE

Embellish a mini-grapevine wreath with leaf clusters to create a napkin ring to accent a harvest table setting. For a special treat, turn it into a party favor for your guest to take home. Simply add a name tag cut from paper or felt, using the pattern below.

Arrange three leaves and tie to grapevine wreath.

Arrange two leaves and tie to grapevine wreath. Tie name tag to wreath, centering it on top of leaves.

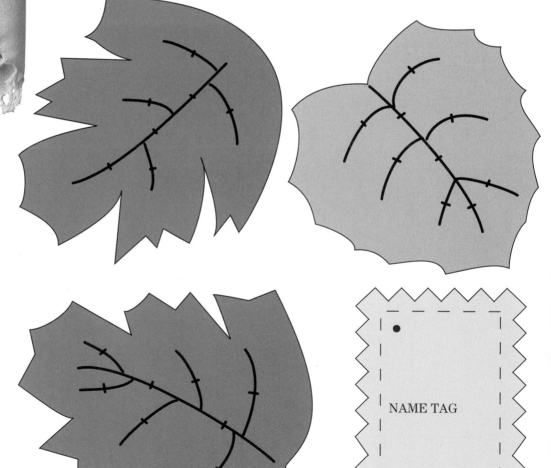

NAME TAG

74

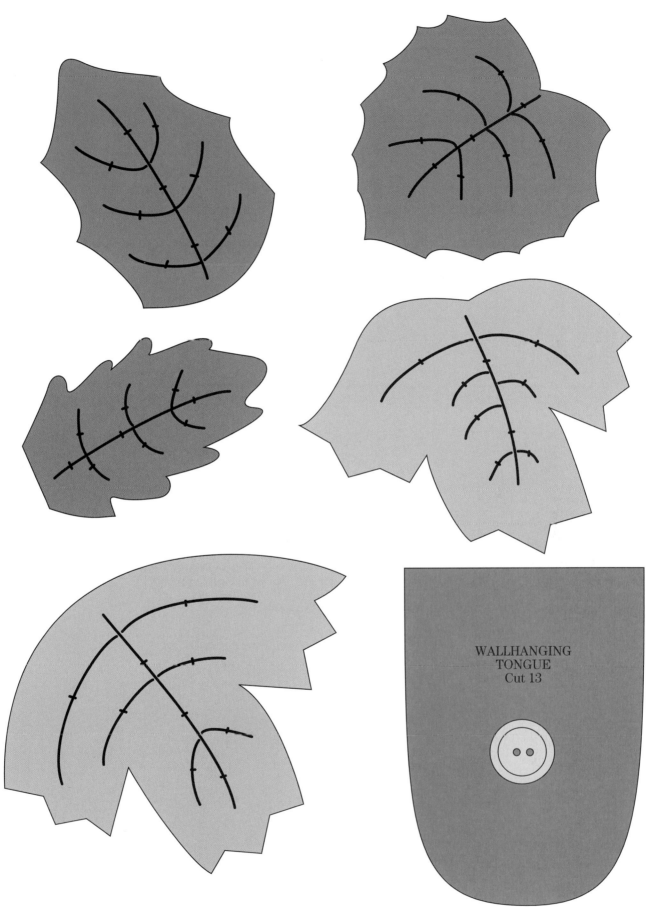

WALLHANGING
TONGUE
Cut 13

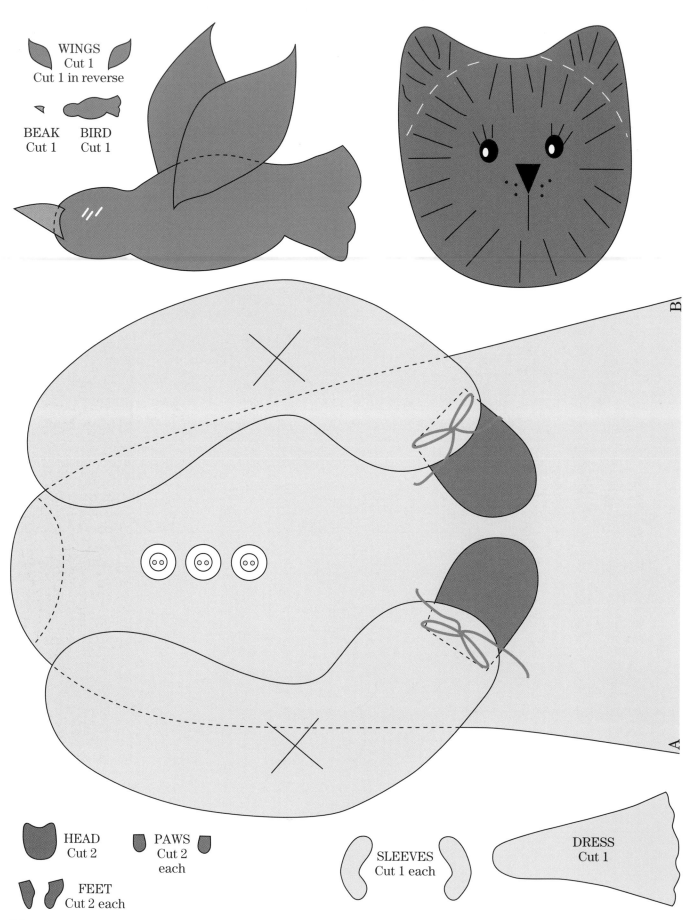

WINGS
Cut 1
Cut 1 in reverse

BEAK
Cut 1

BIRD
Cut 1

B

A

HEAD
Cut 2

PAWS
Cut 2
each

SLEEVES
Cut 1 each

DRESS
Cut 1

FEET
Cut 2 each

76

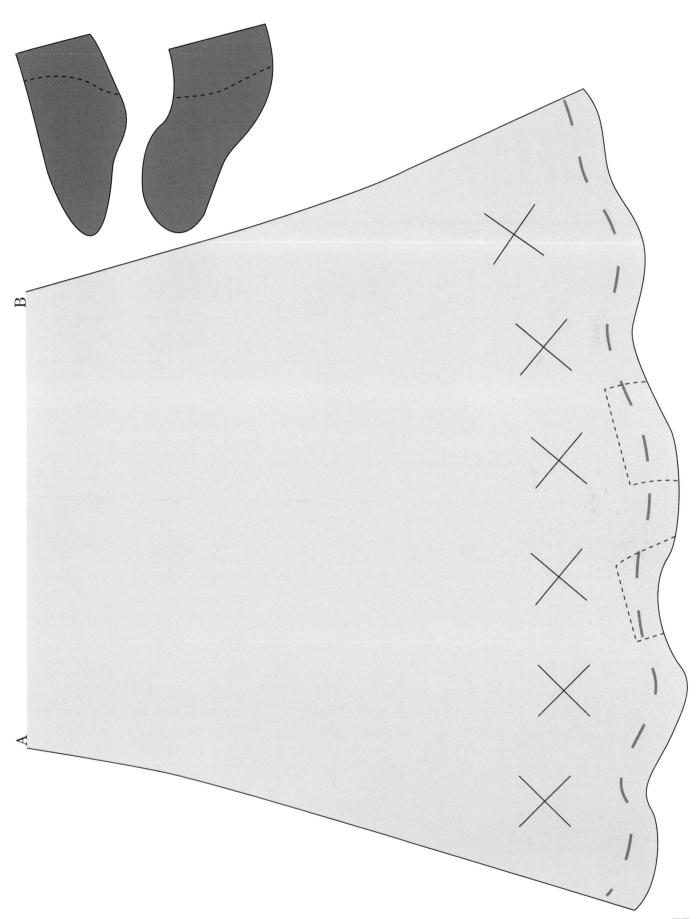

B

A

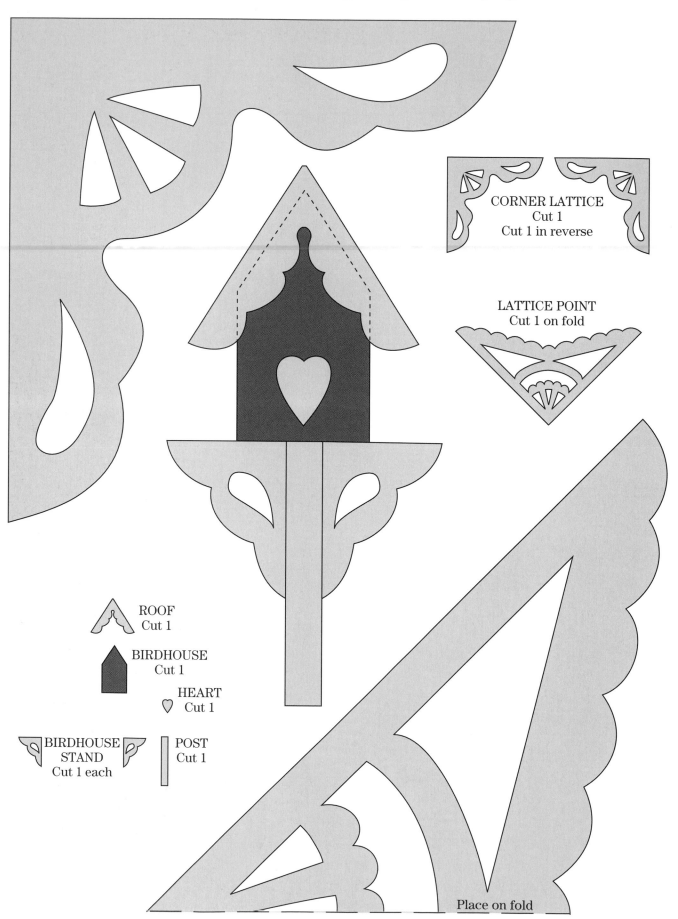

CORNER LATTICE
Cut 1
Cut 1 in reverse

LATTICE POINT
Cut 1 on fold

ROOF
Cut 1

BIRDHOUSE
Cut 1

HEART
Cut 1

BIRDHOUSE
STAND
Cut 1 each

POST
Cut 1

Place on fold

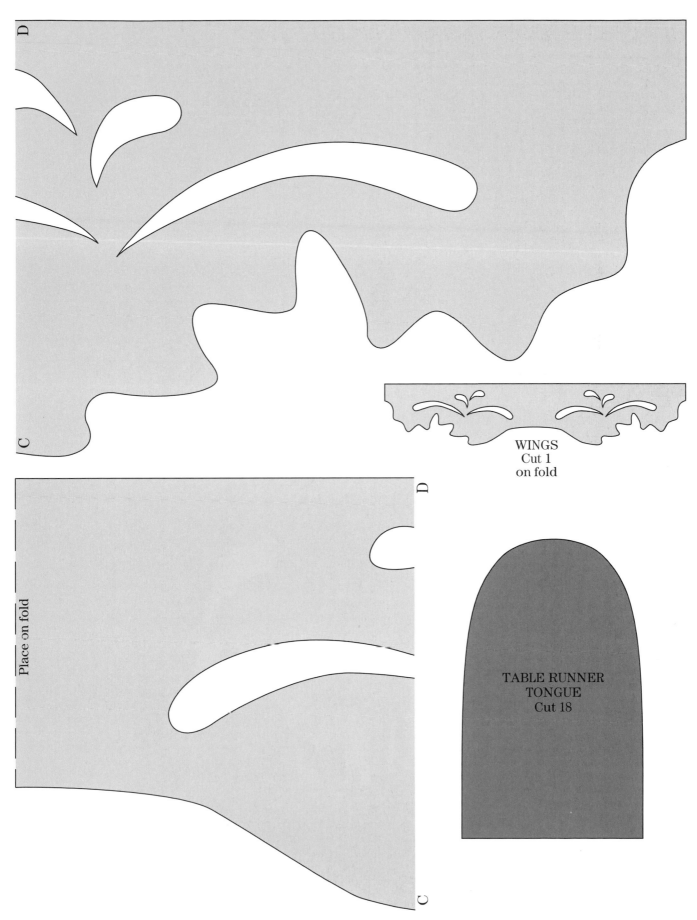

WINGS
Cut 1
on fold

Place on fold

TABLE RUNNER
TONGUE
Cut 18

Holiday Spirit

Nearly 2,000 years ago, love came down at Christmas and the world has been celebrating the birth of a baby born in a manger ever since!

In keeping with these humble circumstances, the rustic felt wallhanging shown *below* reflects the theme "Love Reigns Here," and features a reindeer in a simple woodland setting surrounded by an evergreen-trimmed heart.

Appropriately enough, forest colors of pine green and bark brown are accented with the rich deep hues of burgundy and gold.

The coordinating wool felt stockings are quick-cut with a rotary blade and embellished with festive holly berry hearts. Each stocking sports a charming gift tag with "For You" embroidered with silk ribbon.

To complete the ensemble, a petite tassel-trimmed tree skirt sized for a tabletop tree works up beautifully from burgundy and white wool felt. Finishing touches for the skirt include silk ribbon "branches" embroidered on the alternating heart motifs and tiny heart-shaped charms.

"LOVE REIGNS HERE" WALLHANGING

Wallhanging is 29" high x 29½" wide

For information about materials, tools, techniques, and stitches, read "Tips and Techniques" starting on page 7.

Materials

1 yard of burgundy wool felt for the foreground, hearts, and letters

¾ yard of straw wool felt for the center heart

1 yard of evergreen wool felt for the backing, dark tree, and evergreen Nos. 2 and 4

¼ yard of loden wool felt for the light tree, evergreen border, and evergreen Nos. 1, 3, and 5

¼ yard of light brown wool felt for the deer, tree trunks, and branches

¼ yard of old gold wool felt for the bottom banner, sun, and bow

One 9" x 12" piece of white wool felt for the snow and deer's tail

Size 5 DMC pearl cotton: one ball or two skeins of black (No. 310); one skein or scraps of dark gold (No. 782)

Size 8 DMC pearl cotton: one ball of light tan (No. 738)

2 yards of gold-nugget color Offray 2mm chainette

¼ yard of metallic gold fine braid

No. 20 and No. 22 chenille needles

Mark-B-Gone marking pens: white ink and water-erasable

Pinking shears or Dritz rotary cutter with pinking blade

♥

Prepare Pieces

1. Shrink the wool felt, washing each color separately. Dry in dryer.
2. Referring to the diagram with pattern on page 88, create a full-size large center heart pattern.
3. Draw a 5½"-diameter circle for the full-size sun pattern.
4. Trace the remaining full-size patterns, pages 88-94, joining A to A and B to B to complete the bottom banner, and C to C and D to D to complete the evergreen border. Cut out.
5. Referring to the materials list for the suggested colors and to patterns or diagrams with patterns for numbers, use white ink or water-erasable marker to trace around patterns on felt. Cut out.

   Use embroidery scissors to cut out the center of letters *O* and *R*, and to cut slits in the tree and evergreen pieces where marked.
6. On a large piece of burgundy wool felt, use a white ink or water-erasable marker to draw a 29"-wide x 27"-high rectangle. Cut out, leaving at least a 1½" border all around to be trimmed off later.

   Center the large heart pattern about 4" below the top marked edge of the burgundy felt and trace around the pattern. Cut out heart shape.
7. From the straw wool felt, cut one 22" square. Center the square behind the heart-shaped opening of burgundy piece. Pin in place.

Stitch Center Design

1. Referring to Diagram 1, position snow and sun pieces on heart so edges are overlapped by burgundy felt along dashed lines. Pin in place. Referring to the dashed lines on tree patterns, weave each tree trunk through slits of the matching tree. Position trees on heart so edges are overlapped by burgundy piece. Pin in place.

DIAGRAM 1

2. With light tan pearl cotton on burgundy felt, use long running stitches to outline the heart about ⅝" from the edge.

3. With black pearl cotton, blanket-stitch all exposed edges of the snow and sun. Use irregular straight stitches to attach all exposed edges of the two trees. Secure the point of each tree trunk with a small straight stitch.

4. Referring to Diagram 2, position and pin evergreens around the heart cutout.

5. For the branches, cut two 24" x ⅜" strips of the light brown felt. Weave one strip through slits on evergreen pieces along one side of heart. Weave remaining strip through slits on evergreen pieces along opposite side of heart. Trim the ends at an angle.

6. With black pearl cotton, attach all the exposed edges of evergreen pieces with irregular straight stitches. Secure exposed portions of branches with black French knots, spaced about 1" apart. Blanket-stitch all exposed burgundy edges surrounding the heart.

DIAGRAM 2

7. With black pearl cotton, embroider deer's eyes and attach heart-shaped nose with a French knot and straight stitch as seen on face pattern. Attach deer's white tail with running stitches as seen on body pattern.

8. Referring to Diagram 2, position and pin deer to heart. With black pearl cotton, blanket-stitch all exposed edges of deer.

9. Pin bow under deer's chin. Thread needle with fine metallic braid and take a tiny stitch in the center of the felt bow, leaving two long tails on front of bow. Tie ends into a bow.

Stitch Bottom Banner

1. Pin bottom banner to burgundy piece, matching bottom edge of banner with bottom drawn line. Turn wallhanging over and carefully trim away any excess straw felt behind heart cutout. Trim bottom edge even with bottom of banner. Trim burgundy felt on the drawn lines.

2. Referring to banner diagram and full-size patterns for position, pages 92-93, pin the hearts and letters on the banner. Blanket-stitch in place with light tan pearl cotton.

3. Pin wallhanging, right side up, onto top of a large piece of evergreen wool felt. With light tan pearl cotton and a long running stitch, attach burgundy foreground to evergreen backing along top and side edges about ¼" inside

burgundy edge. Do not stitch the bottom edge.

4. Slip two evergreen borders between the burgundy foreground and evergreen backing, so they are overlapped by the banner at dashed lines. Pin in place. Attach banner with light tan pearl cotton and long running stitches, stitching through all layers about ¼" inside edge of banner.

5. With black pearl cotton, attach all exposed edges of evergreen borders with irregular straight stitches.

6. With dark gold pearl cotton on straw felt, outline sun with a running stitch about ¼" from the edge.

7. Use pinking shears to trim backing, leaving at least a ¼" excess all around.

8. Thread larger chenille needle with a 1-yard length of chainette and knot the end. Pull chainette through felt, coming out on front of wallhanging under lower end of one tree branch.

Referring to photo on page 80, wind chainette around the woven brown branches, leaving a long tail hanging down the center of the heart. Pull chainette through top of one burgundy felt heart; remove needle; and tie a knot. Weave the remaining chainette around the branch on the opposite side of the heart in the same way. Loosely tie the two chainette ends together so they gracefully cascade down the center of the design.

TABLETOP TREE SKIRT

Tree skirt measures 25½" across

For information about the materials, tools, techniques, and stitches, read "Tips and Techniques" starting on page 7.

Materials

1 yard each of burgundy and straw wool felt

Size 5 DMC pearl cotton: one ball or two skeins of black (No. 310)

No. 22 and No. 24 chenille needles

YLI 4mm silk ribbon (A): one 5-yard reel each of golden brown (No. 52), brown (No.67), light teal (No. 131), medium teal (No. 74)

YLI 7mm silk ribbon (B): one 5-yard reel of dark teal (No. 75)

Six brass heart-shaped charms

4 yards of Hollywood Trim 1" tasseled fringe (color 101)

Off-white sewing thread and hand-sewing needle

Template plastic and permanent-ink marker

Mark-B-Gone marking pens: white ink or water-erasable ink

Pinking shears or Dritz rotary cutter with pinking blade

♥

Prepare Pieces

1. Shrink the wool felt, washing each color separately. Dry in dryer.
2. Referring to diagram on page 95, and to full-size patterns on pages 94-95, trace tree skirt pattern onto template plastic. Cut out.
3. On burgundy wool felt, use Mark-B-Gone marker to trace around tree skirt pattern six times, joining C to C and D to D each time, forming a circular design as seen in diagram on page 95. Draw a 3"-diameter circle in center of design. (Adjust size of opening to fit the base of your tabletop tree.)
4. Cut out tree skirt on traced lines. Cut out center circle.

Stitch Tree Skirt

1. From straw wool felt, cut one 28" x 28" square. Center burgundy tree skirt on top and either pin or baste in place.
2. With black pearl cotton and No. 22 chenille needle, sew running stitches around heart-shaped cutouts.
3. With black pearl cotton, blanket-stitch around each fleur-de-lis shape and outer edges of tree skirt.
4. With embroidery scissors, cut out center of straw wool felt. Blanket-stitch edges together with black pearl cotton.
5. Referring to stitch and color guide on page 95, use No. 24 chenille needle to embroider each solid point of tree skirt with silk ribbon as shown on pattern.
6. Hand-sew one brass charm below the center knot of each ribbon bow.

Finish Tree Skirt

1. With pinking shears, cut away the straw felt ¼" beyond the edges of burgundy felt.
2. Hand-sew the edge of the tasseled fringe behind the cut edge of straw felt.

HOLIDAY STOCKINGS
Each stocking is about 15½" long

Note: Variegated pearl cottons (Nos. 92 and 115) can be substituted for the colors listed below.

For information about materials, tools, techniques, and stitches, read "Tips and Techniques" starting on page 7.

Materials

⅜ yard each of light brown or straw wool felt for the stockings, cuffs, stripes, and front of tags

♥

One 9" x 12" piece of burgundy wool felt for the heels, toes, hearts, and back of one tag

♥

One 9" x 12" piece of evergreen wool felt for the holly leaves and back of one tag

♥

Size 8 DMC pearl cotton: one ball each of light green (No. 368), light red (No. 498), dark red (No. 815) (see Note above)

♥

No. 22 and No. 24 chenille needles

♥

YLI 4mm silk ribbon: 24" piece each of burgundy (No. 50), golden brown (No. 52)

♥

Tulip Dimensional Fabric Paint with fine-line tip in any coordinating color for tags

♥

Mark-B-Gone marking pens: white ink and water-erasable ink

♥

Pinking shears or Dritz rotary cutter with pinking blade

♥

Prepare Pieces

1. Shrink the wool felt, washing each color separately. Dry in dryer.
2. Referring to the diagrams with full-size patterns on pages 96-97, trace individual pieces joining A to A and B to B to complete the stocking patterns. Cut out.
3. With Mark-B-Gone marker, trace around the stocking pattern once on either the light brown or the straw wool felt. For the brown stocking, trace around cuff and stripe patterns on straw felt; and for off-white stocking, trace around cuff and stripe patterns on light brown felt.

    For either stocking trace around the heel, toe, and heart patterns on the burgundy felt, and around holly leaf pattern on evergreen felt.

    For each tag, trace around front of tag on straw felt, and back of tag on either burgundy or evergreen felt.
4. Leaving stockings uncut for now, use pinking shears to cut out all remaining pieces.

Stitch Stocking

1. Referring to the full-size pattern for position, pin cuff and stripes on the uncut stocking.
2. Thread smaller chenille needle with either dark or light red pearl cotton and attach cuff with feather stitches along the top edge of cuff. Use the opposite shade of red pearl cotton to embroider feather stitches along the bottom edge of cuff.

    Continuing to alternate the two shades of red pearl cotton, attach each stripe with a row of feather stitches along the center of the stripe.
3. Referring to the pattern for position, pin two holly leaves on the cuff. Stitch leaves in place, using light green pearl cotton and running stitches.

4. Arrange three hearts between two leaves. Use either shade of red pearl cotton to tie the hearts in place, leaving tails that are ½" to 1" long.

5. Referring to pattern for position, pin heel and toe pieces on uncut stocking. Using either shade of red pearl cotton and a running stitch, attach the inside edges to stocking. For next step, use the alternate shade of red.

6. Pin stitched stocking, right side up, on top of an uncut piece of matching color felt. Leaving open at top, sew a running stitch around stocking about ¼" inside traced edges.

7. With pinking shears, cut out stocking through all layers of felt.

Make Tags

1. With marker, print the words "For You" or name of recipient on front of tag.

2. Using a larger chenille needle and either shade of silk ribbon, embroider the letters with outline stitch. If preferred, write the names with dimensional fabric paint instead.

3. Center front of tag, right side up, on top of the back tag. Use either shade of the red pearl cotton to attach front with a border of running stitches.

4. For each tag, cut a 24" piece of either burgundy or golden brown silk ribbon. Fold one length in half. While holding the two loose ends in one hand, hook the fold around a finger on the opposite hand and rotate that finger to twist the ribbon. Continue twisting until the ribbon begins to feel stiff; then, carefully fold this length in half, holding both ends in one hand and letting go of the new fold so the ribbon twists onto itself.

   Tie loose ends with an overhand knot and hand-stitch to back of tag in upper left-hand corner.

5. Hand-sew tag to upper left-hand corner of stocking.

I find that wool felt has the extraordinary capacity for getting all dressed up— making it easier than ever to celebrate with holiday spirit!

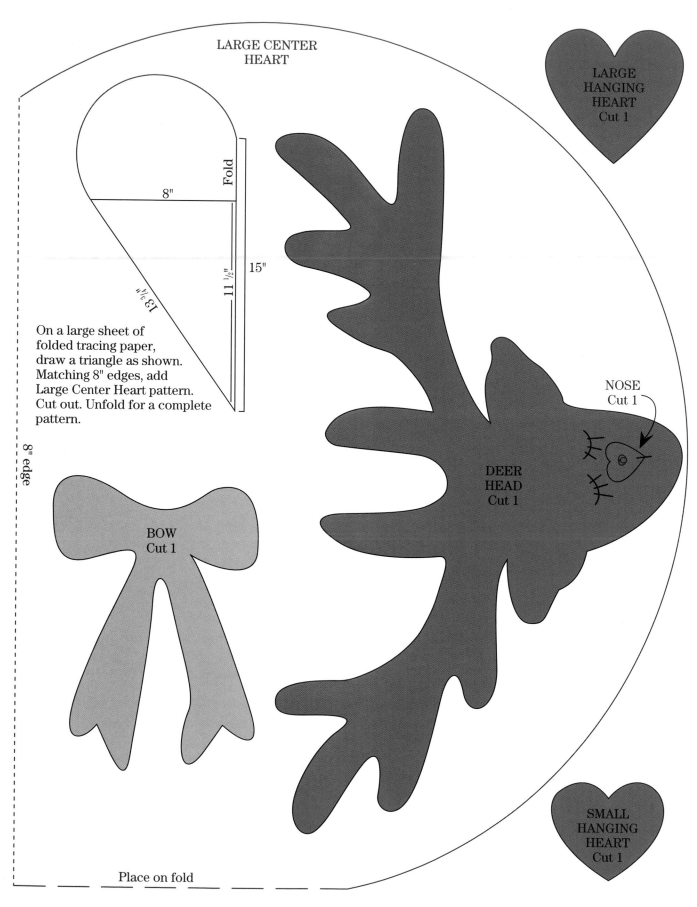

LARGE CENTER
HEART

Fold

8"

15"

11 1/2"

13 3/4"

LARGE
HANGING
HEART
Cut 1

NOSE
Cut 1

DEER
HEAD
Cut 1

On a large sheet of
folded tracing paper,
draw a triangle as shown.
Matching 8" edges, add
Large Center Heart pattern.
Cut out. Unfold for a complete
pattern.

8" edge

BOW
Cut 1

SMALL
HANGING
HEART
Cut 1

Place on fold

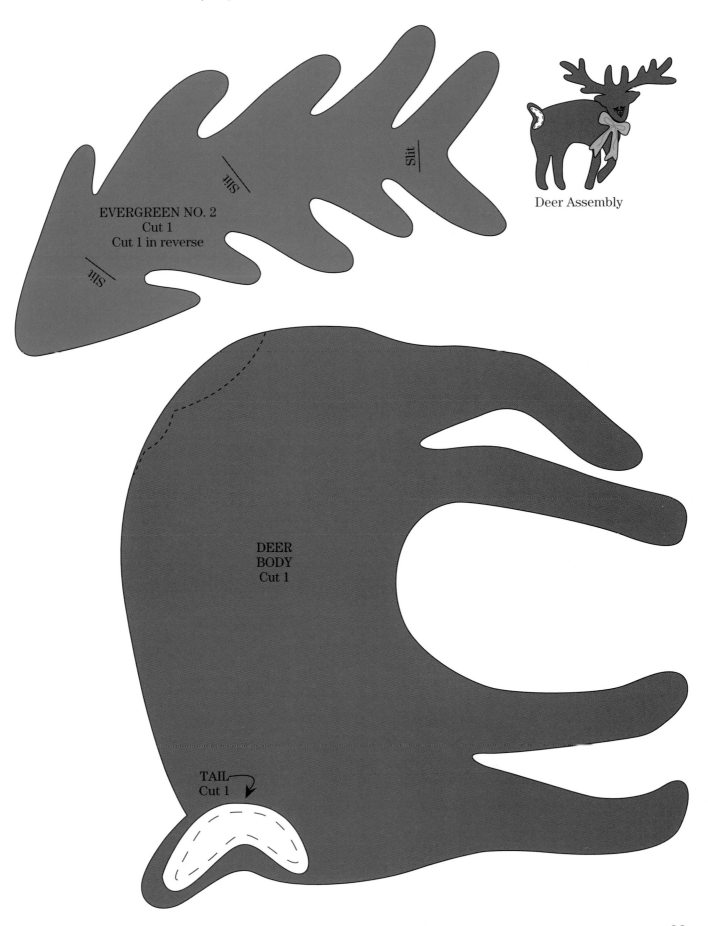

Deer Assembly

EVERGREEN NO. 2
Cut 1
Cut 1 in reverse

Slit

Slit

Slit

DEER
BODY
Cut 1

TAIL
Cut 1

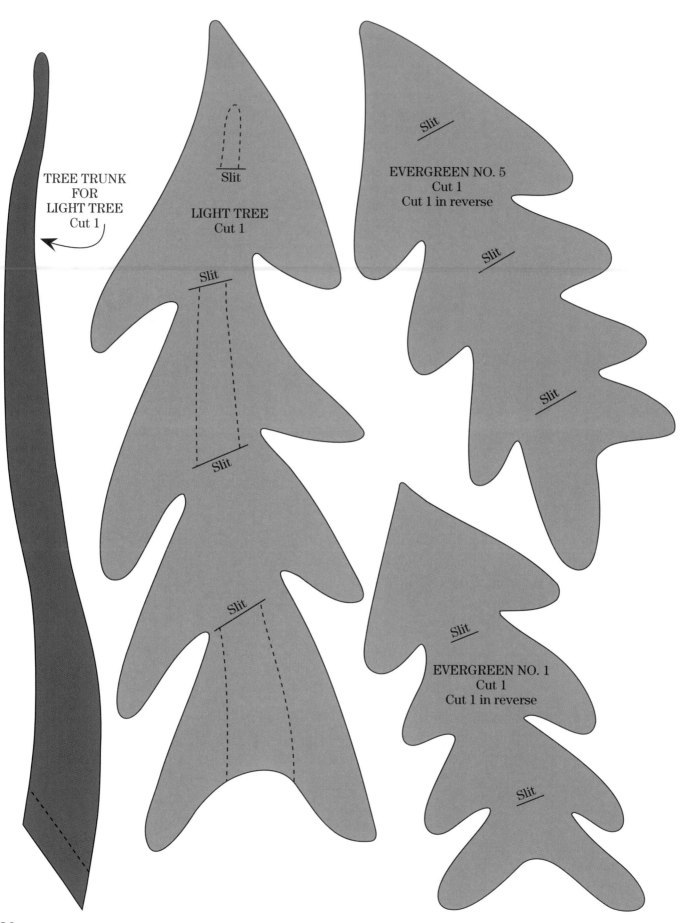

TREE TRUNK
FOR
LIGHT TREE
Cut 1

LIGHT TREE
Cut 1

Slit

Slit

Slit

Slit

EVERGREEN NO. 5
Cut 1
Cut 1 in reverse

Slit

Slit

Slit

EVERGREEN NO. 1
Cut 1
Cut 1 in reverse

Slit

Slit

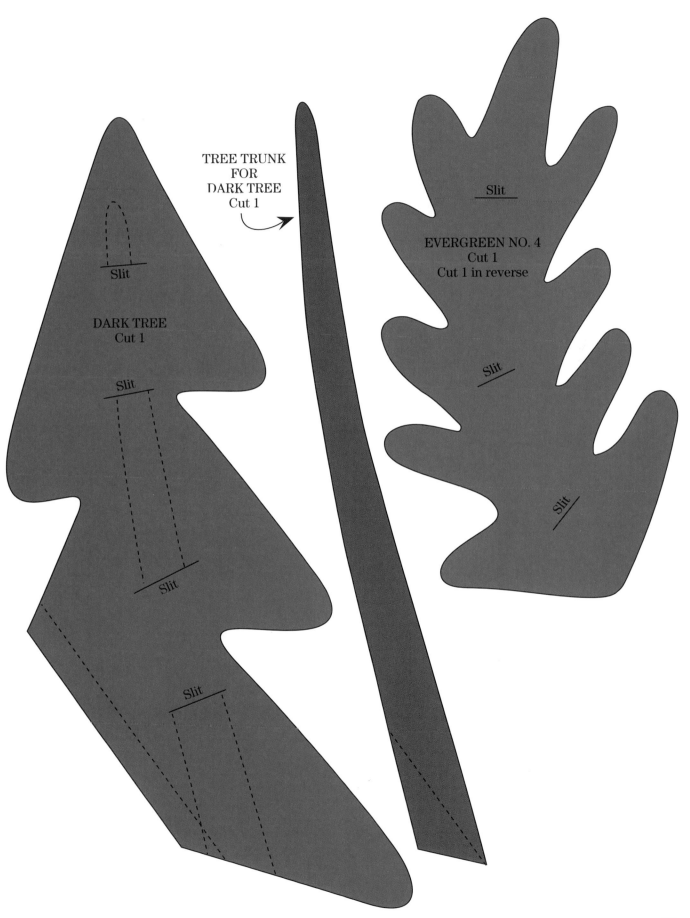

TREE TRUNK
FOR
DARK TREE
Cut 1

Slit

EVERGREEN NO. 4
Cut 1
Cut 1 in reverse

Slit

Slit

Slit

DARK TREE
Cut 1

Slit

Slit

Slit

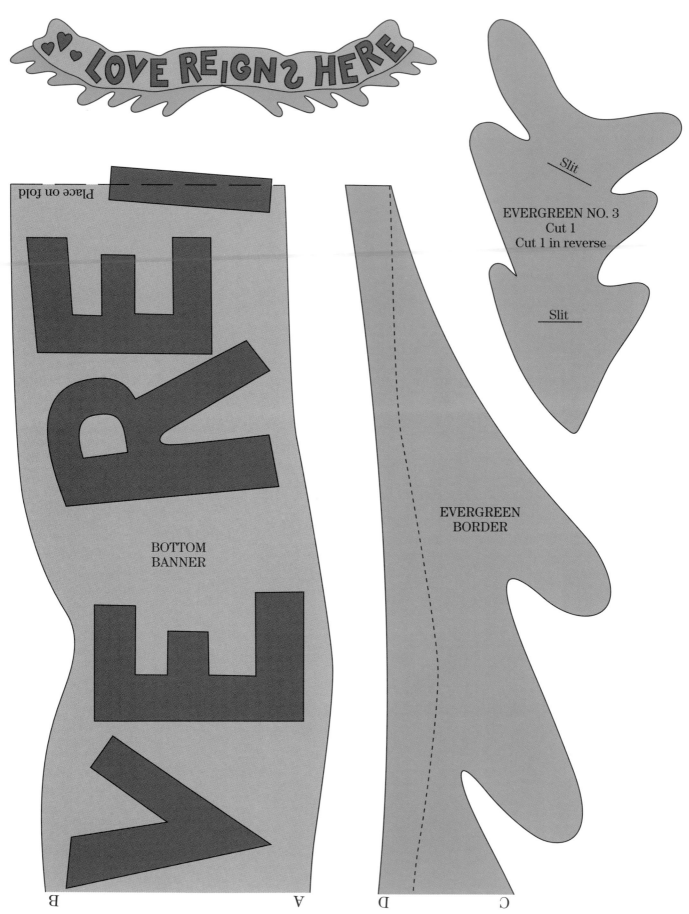

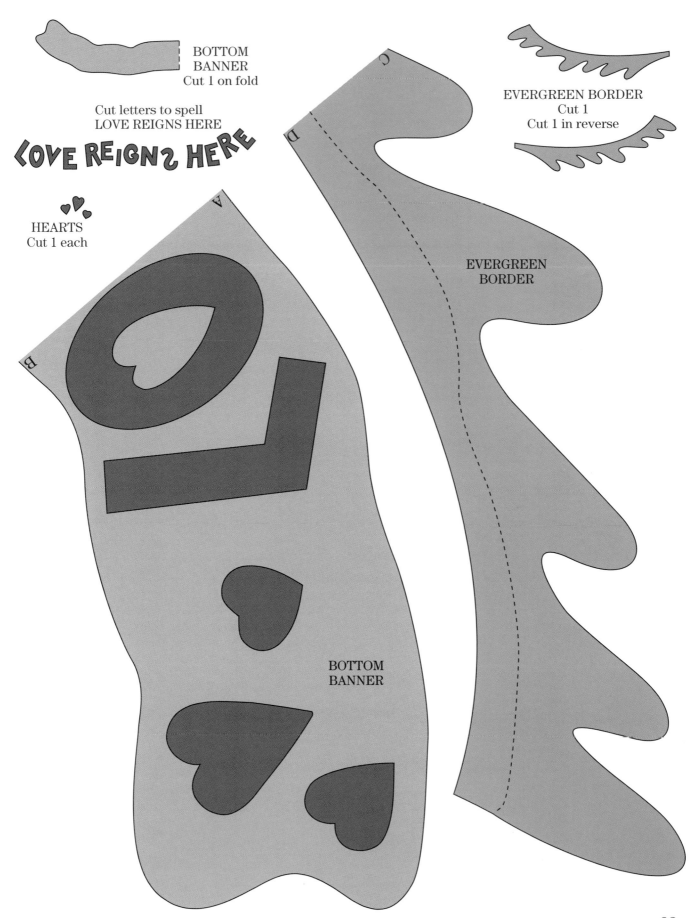

BOTTOM
BANNER
Cut 1 on fold

Cut letters to spell
LOVE REIGNS HERE

HEARTS
Cut 1 each

EVERGREEN BORDER
Cut 1
Cut 1 in reverse

EVERGREEN
BORDER

BOTTOM
BANNER

93

SNOW
Cut 1

Cut out

Cut out

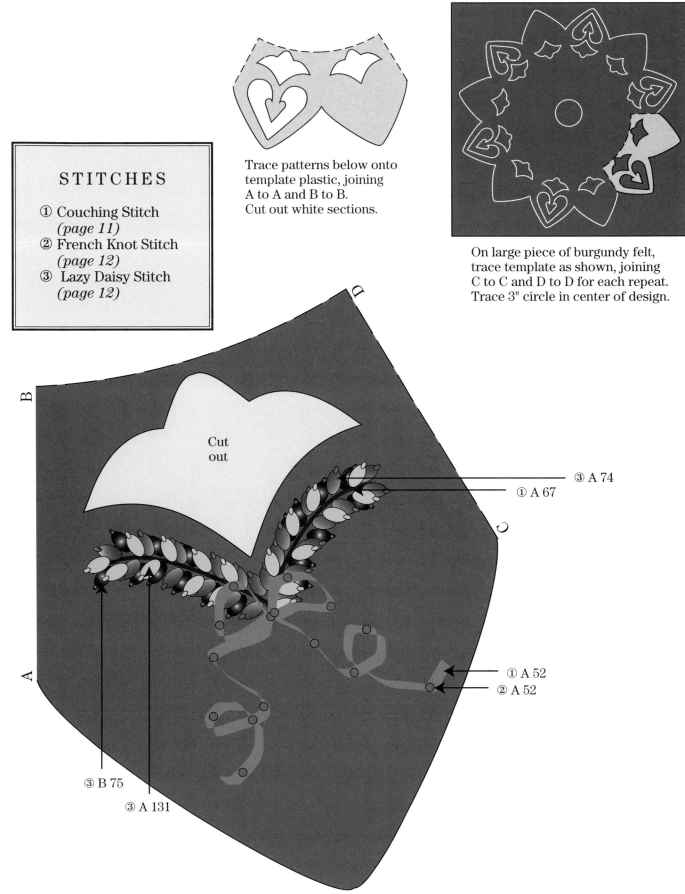

Trace patterns below onto template plastic, joining A to A and B to B. Cut out white sections.

On large piece of burgundy felt, trace template as shown, joining C to C and D to D for each repeat. Trace 3" circle in center of design.

STITCHES

① Couching Stitch
   (page 11)
② French Knot Stitch
   (page 12)
③ Lazy Daisy Stitch
   (page 12)

D

B

C

A

Cut out

③ A 74

① A 67

① A 52

② A 52

③ B 75

③ A 131

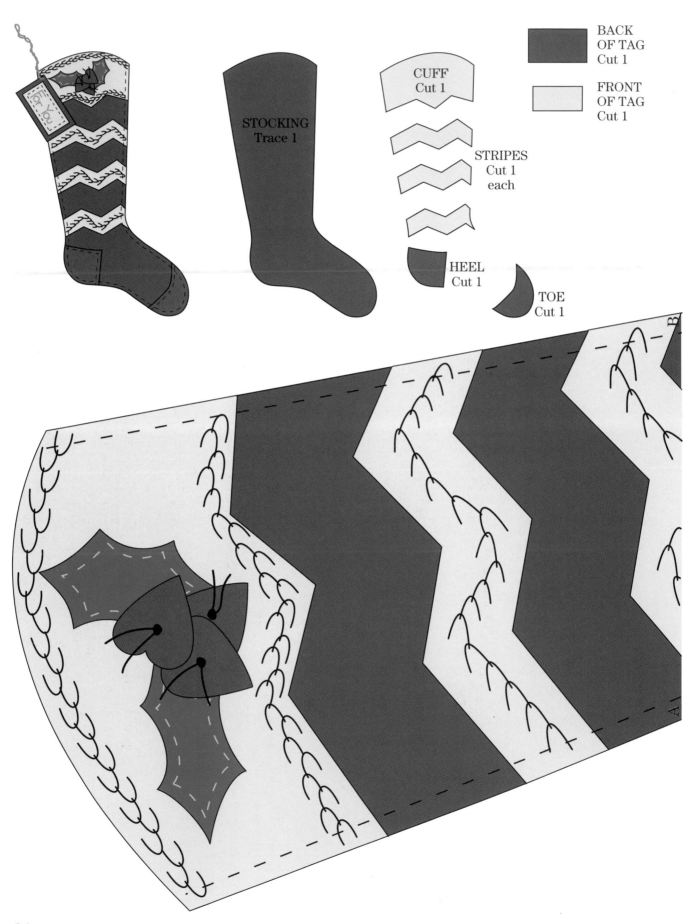

BACK
OF TAG
Cut 1

FRONT
OF TAG
Cut 1

STOCKING
Trace 1

CUFF
Cut 1

STRIPES
Cut 1
each

HEEL
Cut 1

TOE
Cut 1

96

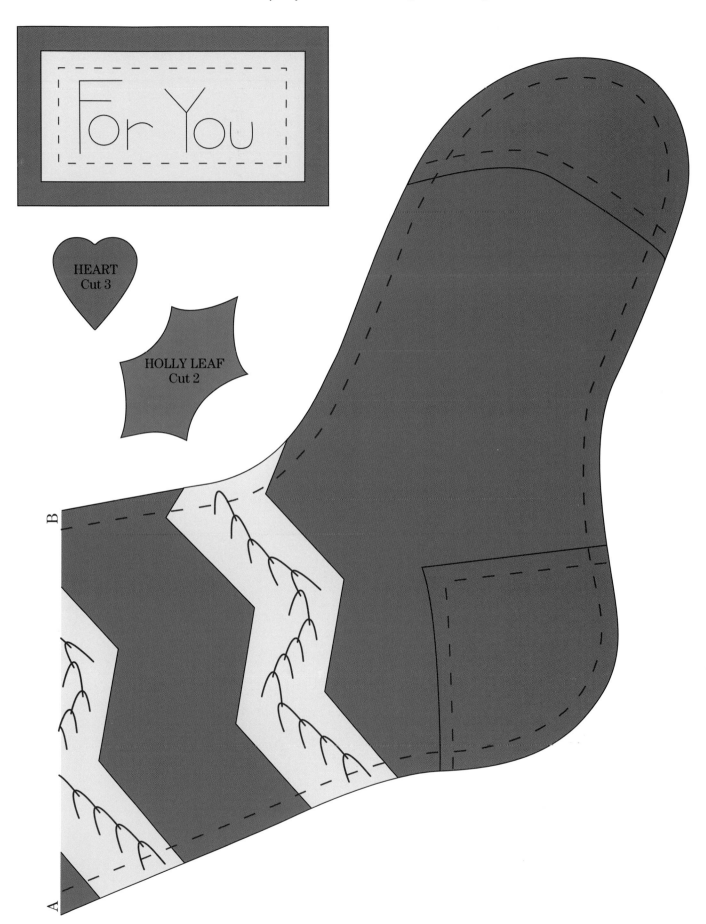

For You

HEART
Cut 3

HOLLY LEAF
Cut 2

B

A

Valentine, Be Mine

"Valentine, Be Mine"—a favorite sentiment found on antique greeting cards —is inspiration for the heartwarming collection of projects to share and wear shown here and on the following pages. The theme is artfully expressed in needlework on the wallhanging, *below,* which features the ribbon-embroidered phrase "Be Mine" surrounded by a bouquet of flowers and fruit.

Other inspirations to share include the lavishly trimmed Valentine pillow, a bead-fringed pin, and a sewing basket cover complete with Cupid's arrow. A companion to the sewing basket, the pincushion cover is brimming with a trio of embroidered blooms that works up quickly with silk ribbon.

Top it all off with something spectacular you'll love to wear—a white wool vest accented with antique pillowcase lace trimmed with a pleasing arrangement of silk ribbons, buttons, and beads.

"BE MINE" WALLHANGING

Wallhanging is 21" wide x 30" long, excluding fringe

For information about materials, tools, techniques, and stitches, including dyed felted wools, read "Tips and Techniques" starting on page 7.

For information about obtaining dyed felted wools see Sources on page 13.

Note: A slice of dyed felted wool measures 6½" x 15½".

Materials

1 yard each of 72"-wide wool felt: blue spruce for the backing, triangles and square; straw for the background

♥

One 9" x 12" piece each of wool felt: light plum for the hearts; loden for leaves (B); Kelly green for leaves (C, E) and sepal (C)

♥

One slice each of felted wools: Boston ivy for the leaves (A); old blue for the pears; ecru for the flowers (B); light lavender for petal (C-2); medium lavender for petals (C-1) and bud (C-3); dark lavender for petals (C-1) and bud (C-4); madder root red for the flowers (D); dark spruce for the leaves (D) and sepal (D); bittersweet for the flowers (E); brass for the flowers (E); light violet for flowers (F) (see Sources on page 13 and Note above)

♥

2mm YLI silk ribbon: two 5-yard reels of ecru (No. 156); one reel each of grass green (No. 20), blue-green (No. 32), blue (No. 45), pale grape (No. 178)

♥

4mm YLI silk ribbon: one 5-yard reel each of very pale yellow (No. 13), yellow (No. 15), blue-green (No. 32), dark tan (No. 36), burgundy (No. 49), dark gold (No. 55), leaf green (No. 61), light copper (No. 76), dark purple (No. 85), coral (No. 88), dusty rose (No. 114), periwinkle (No. 117), copper brown (No. 151), very pale green (No. 154), olive green (No. 171)

♥

7mm YLI silk ribbon: one 5-yard reel each of yellow (No. 15), forest green (No. 75)

♥

No. 24 and No. 26 chenille needles

♥

Off-white and dark red thread

♥

About 3 dozen white antique pearl buttons varying in size from ½" to 1½" in diameter

♥

Antique or new crocheted lace doily to fit within a 9½" x 12" area

♥

1½ yards of 3"-long bullion fringe and matching thread

♥

Mark-B-Gone marking pens: water-erasable or disappearing-ink

♥

Transfer pen or pencil (optional)

♥

Prepare Pieces

1. Shrink the wool felt, washing each color separately. Dry in dryer.
2. Trace the full-size patterns on pages 112-113 onto tracing paper; cut out.
3. From the blue spruce wool felt, cut two small triangles and 11 large triangles. Cut one large triangle on the fold and unfold for a 6" square.
4. Referring to Diagram 1, use a water-erasable marking pen to draw a 20½"-wide x 25"-high rectangle on a large piece of pre-shrunk straw wool felt. Along the bottom 20½" edge, measure and mark the center point and 6" from each corner. Measure 5" down from the center point and join this point with each 6"-mark to create a triangular shape in the center of the bottom edge. Cut out.

Valentine, Be Mine

5. Referring to Diagram 1, position the triangles and square on the straw felt background about ½" in from the edges. Pin in place.

6. Referring to manufacturer's directions, use transfer pen or pencil to transfer lettering to front piece about 1" below triangle 2. If preferred, use the pattern as a guide to hand-print the words instead, using either a water-erasable or disappearing-ink marker.

Attach Triangles

1. For all embroidery, use the smaller needle for 2mm and 4mm ribbons and the larger needle for 7mm ribbons. The recommended ribbons and stitches can be changed to suit your taste.

2. Referring to Diagram 1 for position, attach triangle 1 with the No. 55 4mm ribbon and large cross-stitches; triangle 2 with No. 114 4mm ribbon and double feather stitches; and triangle 3 with No. 117 4mm ribbon and feather stitches.

3. Continuing down the right side, attach triangle 4 with No. 154 4mm ribbon and herringbone stitches; triangle 5 with No. 88 4mm ribbon and large cross-stitches; triangle 6 with No. 178 2mm ribbon and wavy blanket stitches; and triangle 7 with No. 45 2mm ribbon and feather stitches.

4. Continuing across the bottom, attach triangle 8 with No. 13 4mm ribbon and feather stitches; square 9 with No. 156 2mm ribbon and herringbone stitches; and triangle 10 with No. 36 4mm ribbon and herringbone stitches.

5. Finishing up the side, attach triangle 11 with No. 154 4mm ribbon and wavy blanket stitches; triangle 12 with No. 45 2mm ribbon and feather stitches; triangle 13 with No. 13 4mm ribbon and feather stitches; and triangle 14 with No. 49 4mm ribbon and herringbone stitches.

Attach Pears

1. From old blue felted wool, cut four pears. From Boston ivy felted wool, cut three A leaves. Embroider the veins on the leaves with No. 75 7mm ribbon and stem stitches.

2. Referring to the diagram on page 113, arrange the pears and leaves across triangles 1-4. Attach pears with No. 45 2mm blue ribbon and blanket stitches. Attach leaves with No. 75 7mm ribbon and running stitches.

3. For the vine, gracefully weave No. 75 7mm ribbon in and out of triangles 1-4, joining the tops of each leaf and pear. Use a couching stitch to hold the ribbon in place every 1" to 1½".

Attach Flowers

1. B Flowers: From ecru felted wool, cut two B flowers. From loden wool felt, cut two B leaves. Referring to pattern for position, fill the center of each flower with No. 15 7mm French knots.

   Referring to the diagram with patterns on page 112, arrange the B

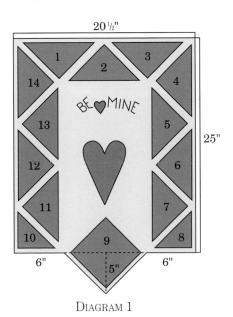

DIAGRAM 1

flowers and leaves across triangles 5 and 6. With a marker, draw the stems.

Attach flowers with No. 156 2mm ribbon and blanket stitches. Embroider the stems with No. 20 2mm ribbon and stem stitches. Attach the leaves with No. 20 2mm ribbon and running stitches.

2. C Flowers: From dark lavender felted wool, cut two C-1 petals and one C-4 bud. From medium lavender felted wool, cut two C-1 petals and one C-3 bud. From light lavender felted wool, cut one C-2 petal. From Kelly green wool felt, cut one C leaf and one C sepal.

Referring to the diagram on page 112, arrange the C flower petals and leaf, and the bud petals and sepal on triangle 7. The dashed lines on patterns show where the pieces overlap. With a marker, draw the stems.

Attach all exposed edges of flower petals and buds with No. 85 4mm ribbon and blanket stitches. Embroider stems with No. 61 4mm ribbon and stem stitches. Attach leaf and sepal with No. 61 4mm ribbon and running stitches.

Working outward from the center with No. 85 4mm ribbon, add several long straight stitches to center of flower. On top of these stitches, add several short straight stitches with No. 15 4mm ribbon.

3. D Flowers: From madder root red felted wool, cut one ½" x 4" strip, one ⅝" x 8" strip, and one ⅝" x 12" strip. From dark spruce felted wool, cut one C leaf and one D sepal. Embroider a vein on the leaf with No. 171 4mm ribbon and stem stitches.

With matching thread, hand-sew zig-zag stitches along one long edge of the 12" strip. Pull thread to gather the edge, forming a circular piece with points. Fasten off thread. Repeat this step with each of two remaining strips,

pulling thread taut enough to close up circles before fastening off the thread.

Pin the large gathered circle on left-hand side of square 9. Pin the medium gathered circle on top so it covers the open center of the large circle. Referring to the photo of the wallhanging for help with the position, slip the leaf under the flower. Next, pin the small gathered circle to the right of the flower for a bud, and overlap its bottom edge with the top edge of the sepal. With a marker, draw the stems, attaching stem of bud to flower stem.

Attach leaf and sepal with No. 171 4mm ribbon and running stitches. Attach the flowers with No. 114 4mm ribbon and randomly placed French knots. Embroider the stems with No. 171 4mm ribbon and stem stitches.

4. E Flowers: From bittersweet and brass felted wools, cut two E flowers of each color. Cut out V-shaped notches along edges of each circle as shown on pattern. From straw wool felt, cut two E flower centers. From Kelly green wool felt, cut two E leaves. Embroider a vein on each leaf with No. 61 4mm ribbon and stem stitch.

Referring to the diagram on page 112, arrange the E flowers and leaves on triangle 12 with darker fabric on top of one flower and lighter fabric on top of the other. Offset the petals and place a small felt circle in the center of each flower.

With a No. 76 4mm ribbon and stitching through all layers, attach flowers by working a cluster of seven French knots in the center of each felt circle. Fill in the circle with French knots, using No. 15 4mm ribbon. Attach leaves with No. 61 4mm ribbon and running stitches.

5. F Flowers: From the light violet felted wool, cut one of each flower. Referring to the diagram on page 112, arrange the flowers on triangle 13. With a marker, add stems.

Referring to patterns for position, use No. 151 4mm ribbon to fill the flower centers with French knots, stitching through all layers. With No. 178 2mm ribbon, blanket-stitch all exposed edges of the flower petals. With No. 20 2mm ribbon, embroider the stems with stem stitches.

6. Referring to instructions for D Flowers in step 3, make two flowers and one bud. Cut two E leaves and one D sepal from dark spruce felted wool. Embroider a vein on each leaf with No. 171 4mm ribbon and stem stitches.

Referring to photo of wallhanging for help with placement, arrange the flowers and bud on triangle 14. With a marker, draw short stems, connecting the flowers.

Attach leaves and sepal with No. 171 4mm ribbon and running stitches. Attach flowers with No. 114 4mm ribbon and randomly placed French knots. Embroider stems with No. 171 4mm ribbon and stem stitches.

Center of Wallhanging

1. Stem-stitch the transferred letters with No. 32 2mm ribbon. Blanket-stitch the small heart in place with No. 156 2mm ribbon.

2. Arrange a lace doily in the center of the wallhanging, and pin the large heart in the center of the doily. With No. 32 4mm ribbon, attach the doily with randomly placed French knots. Blanket-stitch heart in place with No. 156 2mm ribbon.

Finish Wallhanging

1. Cut out straw background fabric on drawn lines. Use water to remove any remaining lines that show.

2. Position the wallhanging on top of blue spruce felt for backing. With No. 156 2mm ribbon and running stitches, attach the edges of the wallhanging to the backing fabric.

3. Cut out the blue spruce felt about ¼" beyond the edges of the straw felt.

4. Referring to the photo for help with placement, arrange the buttons on the wallhanging Attach buttons with No. 32 2mm ribbon.

5. Double the bullion fringe and hand-sew the top edge behind the bottom edge of the wallhanging.

Combining the all-new wool felt and felted wool—accented with silk ribbon embroidery—creates endless colorful possibilities for everything from wallhangings to wearables.

RIBBON-EMBROIDERED WOOL VEST

Vest shown is a woman's size Small

Note: Two pieces of antique crocheted pillowcase lace were used in this project. If similar lace cannot be found, improvise with whatever new or antique lace pieces are available to create a pleasing arrangement.

White or new doilies can be "aged" by dipping them in tea or coffee.

For information about materials, tools, techniques, and stitches, read "Tips and Techniques" starting on page 7.

Materials

Straw-color wool felt vest from National Nonwovens (see Sources on page 13)

♥

2mm YLI silk ribbon (C): two 5-yard reels each of yellow (No. 15); blue-green (No. 33); blue (No. 46); green (No. 60); and three 5-yard reels of ecru (No. 156)

♥

4mm YLI silk ribbon (A): two 5-yard reels each of light yellow (No. 14); brown (No. 36); burgundy (No. 50); dark gold (No. 55); light dusty rose (No. 112); medium dusty rose (No. 113); dusty rose (No. 114); medium blue (No. 126)

♥

7mm YLI silk ribbon (B): two 5-yard reels each of pale dusty rose (No. 111), light blue (No. 125); grape (No. 179)

♥

No. 24 and No. 26 chenille needles

♥

About 2 dozen white antique pearl buttons varying in size from ¼" to 1¼" in diameter

♥

Antique pillowcase lace (see Note above)

♥

1 yard of lightweight fabric for lining

♥

Prepare Pieces

1. Shrink the lining fabric. Dry in dryer.
2. On vest, remove stitching from shoulder seams so vest lays flat and use it as a pattern to cut lining fabric.
3. Re-sew shoulder seams on felt vest. With right sides together, sew shoulder seams on lining. Set lining aside.
4. Turn under all raw edges of vest ½", including armholes, and hand-sew in place using 2mm off-white silk ribbon and long running stitches.

Stitch Design

1. Arrange the lace pieces on the vest. Pin in place. The pieces will be secured by your ribbon embroidery, but if desired, they can first be tacked in place using a matching color thread.

   Attach the long, straight edge of each lace piece with 2mm silk ribbon and long running stitches. Attach the points with French knots, using either a matching color silk ribbon or several coordinating colors.
2. Referring to the stitch guide opposite, embroider the silk ribbon designs among the threads of the crocheted lace. Use the design, opposite, for both the right and left vest front, or vary the design imaginatively, referring to the photo.

   Use the No. 26 chenille needle for 2mm and 4mm ribbons and the No. 24 needle for 7mm ribbons.
   Note: If desired, the large dusty rose flowers may be made from 15" strips of wool felt similar to the D Flowers on the wallhanging (see page 102).
3. Arrange a variety of buttons on vest in a pleasing design. Stitch in place with matching silk ribbon.

Finish Vest

1. With wrong sides together, insert lining. Turn under edges ½" and whipstitch to the edges of vest, using matching thread.

Valentine, Be Mine

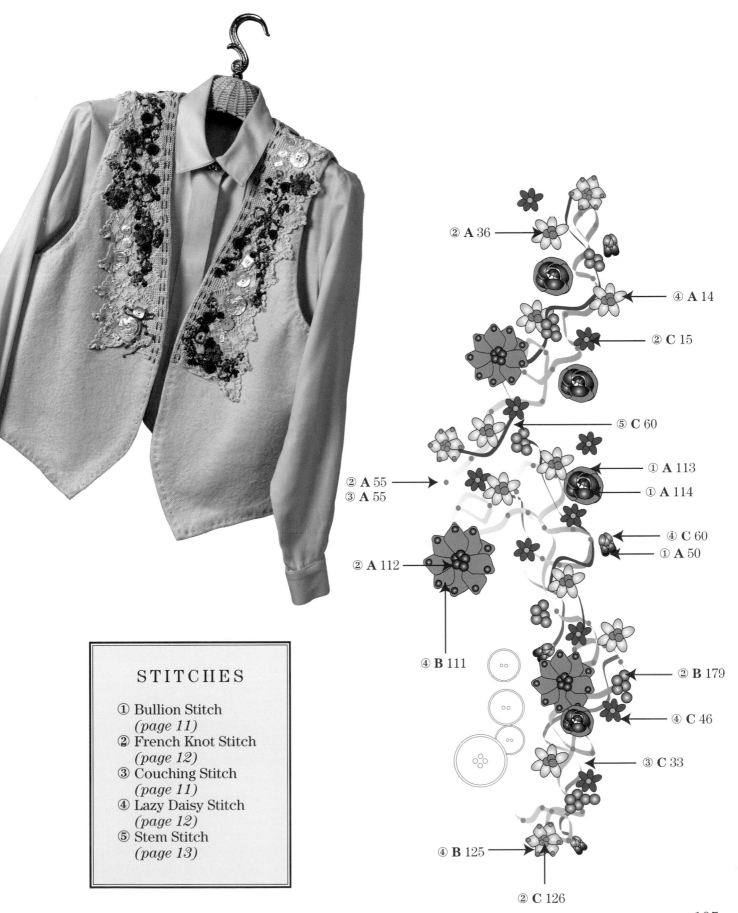

② **A** 36

④ **A** 14

② **C** 15

⑤ **C** 60

② **A** 55
③ **A** 55

① **A** 113
① **A** 114

④ **C** 60
① **A** 50

② **A** 112

④ **B** 111

② **B** 179

④ **C** 46

③ **C** 33

④ **B** 125

② **C** 126

STITCHES

① Bullion Stitch
   (page 11)
② French Knot Stitch
   (page 12)
③ Couching Stitch
   (page 11)
④ Lazy Daisy Stitch
   (page 12)
⑤ Stem Stitch
   (page 13)

VALENTINE PILLOW

*Pillow is 7" high x 8½" wide,
excluding fringe*

For information about the materials, tools, techniques, and stitches used, read "Tips and Techniques" starting on page 7.

Materials

Three 9" x 12" pieces of straw wool felt
for the pillow and small heart

One 9" x 12" piece of evergreen wool felt
for the large heart

YLI 2mm silk ribbon (C): one 5-yard reel
each of yellow (No. 15), blue-green
(No. 33), ecru (No. 156)

YLI 4mm silk ribbon (A): one 5-yard reel
each of brown (No. 37), blue (No. 46),
dusty rose (No. 114)

YLI 7mm silk ribbon (B): one 5-yard reel
each of yellow (No. 15), grape (No. 179)

No. 24 and No. 26 chenille needles

1 yard of yellow-gold chenille fringe trim

Five antique two-hole buttons varying in size
from ⅝" to 1½"

6" x 7½" antique or new lace doily

Polyester fiberfill

Mark-B-Gone marking pens: white ink and
water-erasable ink

Prepare Pieces

1. Shrink the wool felt, washing each color separately. Dry in dryer.
2. Referring to diagrams with full-size patterns opposite, trace the individual pieces onto tracing paper. Cut out.
3. Trace around the patterns on felt with a water-erasable or white ink marker. Leave the large heart uncut. Cut out the small heart.
4. From remaining straw wool felt, cut two 8½" x 10" rectangles for pillow.

Stitch Design

1. Center and baste the smaller heart on the uncut large heart.
2. Referring to the stitch guide opposite, embroider the silk ribbon design along the edges of small heart. Use the No. 26 chenille needle for 2mm and 4mm ribbons and the No. 24 needle for 7mm ribbons.
3. Carefully cut out the large heart.
4. Place the doily at an angle in center of one 8½" x 10" piece of straw wool felt. Place the embroidered heart on the doily at a different angle. Pin in place.
5. Going through all layers, attach the heart to the doily and the straw felt rectangle with the off-white 2mm silk ribbon and herringbone stitches.

Finish Pillow

1. Pin remaining 8½" x 10" straw wool rectangle to embroidered rectangle. Using a ½" seam allowance and leaving an opening on one long side for turning, machine-sew the two pieces together, rounding the corners.
2. Turn pillow and insert stuffing. Turn in raw edges and whipstitch closed.
3. Thread needle with a long length of off-white 2mm silk ribbon. Place a large two-hole button in the center of the embroidered heart. Leaving a long tail on front, sew through one hole of the

Valentine, Be Mine

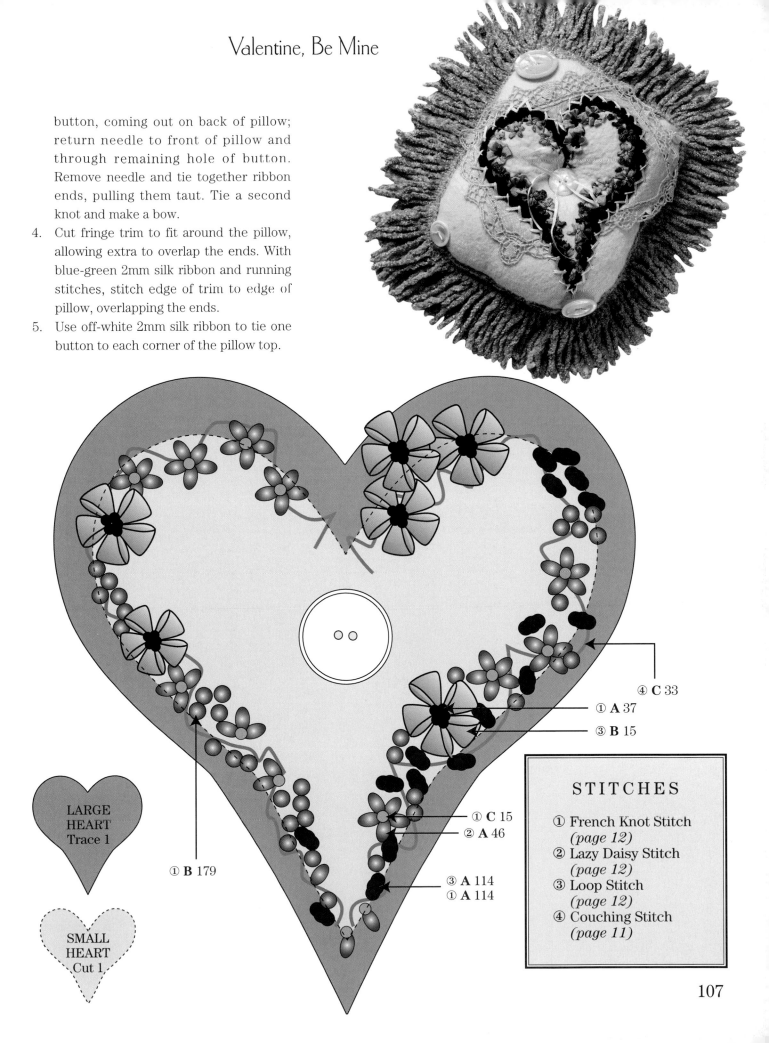

button, coming out on back of pillow; return needle to front of pillow and through remaining hole of button. Remove needle and tie together ribbon ends, pulling them taut. Tie a second knot and make a bow.

4. Cut fringe trim to fit around the pillow, allowing extra to overlap the ends. With blue-green 2mm silk ribbon and running stitches, stitch edge of trim to edge of pillow, overlapping the ends.

5. Use off-white 2mm silk ribbon to tie one button to each corner of the pillow top.

LARGE
HEART
Trace 1

SMALL
HEART
Cut 1

① B 179

④ C 33

① A 37

③ B 15

① C 15

② A 46

③ A 114

① A 114

STITCHES

① French Knot Stitch
(page 12)
② Lazy Daisy Stitch
(page 12)
③ Loop Stitch
(page 12)
④ Couching Stitch
(page 11)

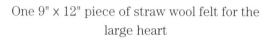

"BE MINE" SEWING BASKET COVER

Design is 7" high x 10" wide

For information about the materials, tools, techniques, and stitches, read "Tips and Techniques" starting on page 7.

Materials

Shaker Sisters Oval Sewing Box with swing handle from Sudberry House, No. 99671 (see Sources on page 13)

♥

One 9" x 12" piece of straw wool felt for the large heart

♥

One 9" x 12" piece or scraps of blue spruce wool felt for the banner

♥

One 9" x 12" piece or scraps of light plum wool felt for the small heart

♥

One 9" x 12" piece or scraps of antique gold wool felt for the arrow

♥

One 12" x 15" piece of any coordinating cotton print for the background

♥

Size 5 DMC pearl cotton: one skein of gold (No. 783)

♥

Size 8 DMC pearl cotton: one ball of pink (No. 605)

♥

No. 22 and No. 26 chenille needles

♥

YLI 4mm silk ribbon (A): one 5-yard reel each of light blue (No. 10), yellow (No. 15), green (No. 19), rose (No. 123)

♥

Nine antique buttons varying in size from ½" to ¾"

♥

1 yard of gimp trim in color that coordinates with fabrics

♥

One 8" x 11" piece of quilt batting

♥

Mark-B-Gone marking pens: water-erasable ink or disappearing-ink

♥

Prepare Pieces

1. Shrink the wool felt, washing each color separately. Dry in dryer.
2. Referring to the full-size pattern opposite, trace the large heart, small heart, banner, and two arrow pieces onto tracing paper. Cut out.
3. Referring to materials list for suggested colors, trace around patterns on felt with a water-erasable marker. Cut out small heart and two arrow pieces. Do not cut out banner and large heart.
4. Use transfer pen or pencil to transfer lettering to banner.

Stitch Design

1. Stem-stitch the letters on the banner with gold pearl cotton. Dot the *i* with a French knot. Cut out banner.
2. Pin the banner, small heart and two arrow pieces onto the large heart. The dashed lines on the patterns show where the pieces overlap.
3. With gold pearl cotton, blanket-stitch the banner and small heart in place. Attach arrow pieces with gold running stitches.
4. Referring to the stitch guide, use No. 26 chenille needle to embroider the silk ribbon design on the small heart.
5. On center of 12" x 15" piece of fabric, trace around full-size oval pattern that comes with sewing box. Cut out large felt heart and center it on the oval. Blanket-stitch around the heart with pink pearl cotton.

Valentine, Be Mine

Be Mine

② **A** 19

② **A** 123

① **A** 15

① **A** 10

6. With the gold pearl cotton, sew one button to the bottom of banner and add a hanging loop to top of small heart.

7. Referring to the pattern, sew three buttons to the large heart and add buttons to the background fabric in small clusters.

Finish Sewing Box

1. Cut batting to fit mounting board for the sewing basket. Place batting on top of mounting board; hand-sew stitched fabric to mounting board. Glue mounting board to cover.

2. Glue the gimp trim around the edge of the cover.

STITCHES

① French Knot Stitch
    (page 12)
② Lazy Daisy Stitch
    (page 12)

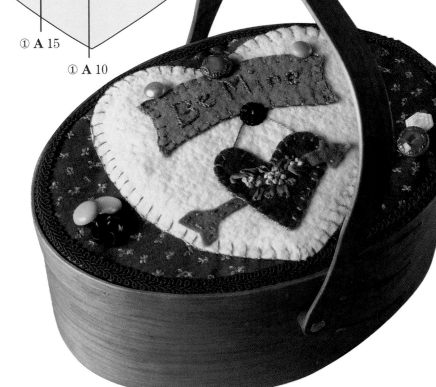

RIBBON-EMBROIDERED PINCUSHION

Design is about 1½" high x 4" wide
Pincushion measures 3" x 4½" oval x 1"
deep with a 3" x 4½" design area

For information about materials, tools, techniques, and stitches, read "Tips and Techniques" starting on page 7.

Materials

Shaker Oval Pincushion from Sudberry House, No. 99651 (see Sources on page 13)

❤

One 9" x 12" piece of straw wool felt for the background

❤

YLI 4mm silk ribbon (A): one 5-yard reel each of white (No. 1), yellow (No. 15), olive green (No. 20), blue-green (No. 33), dusty rose (No. 114), blue (No. 126), burgundy (No. 129), grape (No. 179)

❤

YLI 7mm silk ribbon (B): one 5-yard reel of burgundy (No. 129)

❤

No. 24 and No. 26 chenille needles

❤

½ yard of pink gimp trim

❤

Mark-B-Gone marking pens: water-erasable ink or disappearing-ink

❤

Prepare Pieces

1. Shrink the wool felt. Dry in dryer.
2. Referring to full-size pattern opposite, trace oval onto tracing paper. Cut out.
3. Using a water-erasable or disappearing-ink marker, trace around the oval in center of straw wool felt. Do not cut out.

Stitch Design

1. Referring to the stitch guide, use No. 26 and 24 chenille needles to embroider the silk ribbon design in the center of the oval.
2. Cut out oval shape from felt.

Finish Pincushion

1. Following manufacturer's directions, hand-sew stitched felt to pincushion's padded mounting board. Glue mounting board to wood base.
2. Arrange gimp trim around edge of stitched piece, cutting off the excess after allowing for a small overlap. Glue trim in place, turning under top raw edge at the overlap.

Valentine, Be Mine

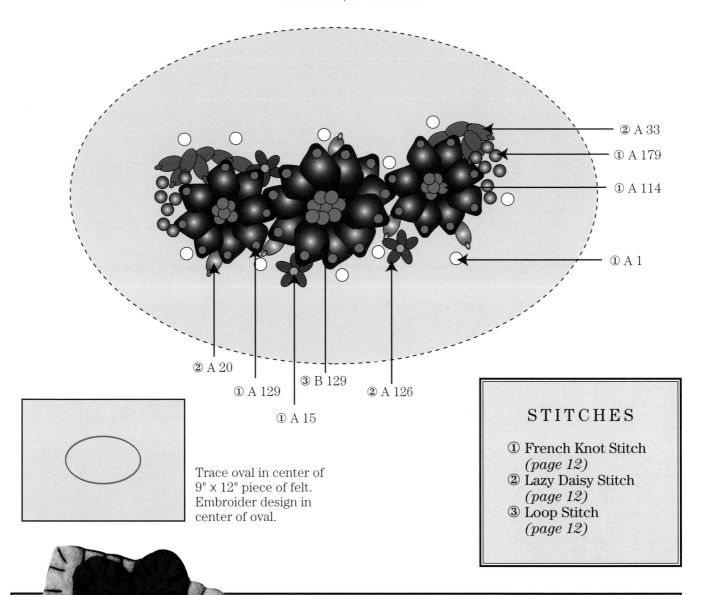

② A 33

① A 179

① A 114

① A 1

② A 20

① A 129

③ B 129

② A 126

① A 15

Trace oval in center of
9" x 12" piece of felt.
Embroider design in
center of oval.

STITCHES

① **French Knot Stitch**
   (page 12)
② **Lazy Daisy Stitch**
   (page 12)
③ **Loop Stitch**
   (page 12)

VALENTINE PIN

Have fun with scraps from your sewing basket! This

Valentine pin makes a great gift or fun fashion accent. Using

the full-size pattern, cut background pieces, one from blue felt and

one from black felt. Cut the heart from red felt. Blanket-

stitch all the pieces together. Embellish with beads and

add a 1½" pin back to the back.

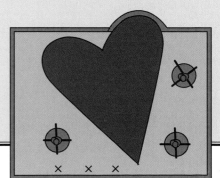

French
knots

FLOWER
F-1

French
knots

FLOWER
F-3

FLOWER
E

Cut
out

13

12

LEAF
E

French
knots

FLOWER
F-2

FLOWER
CENTER
E

5

6

7

FLOWER
B

French
knots

LEAF
C

PETAL
C-1

PETAL
C-2

BUD
C-3

SEPAL
C

LEAF
B

BUD
C-4

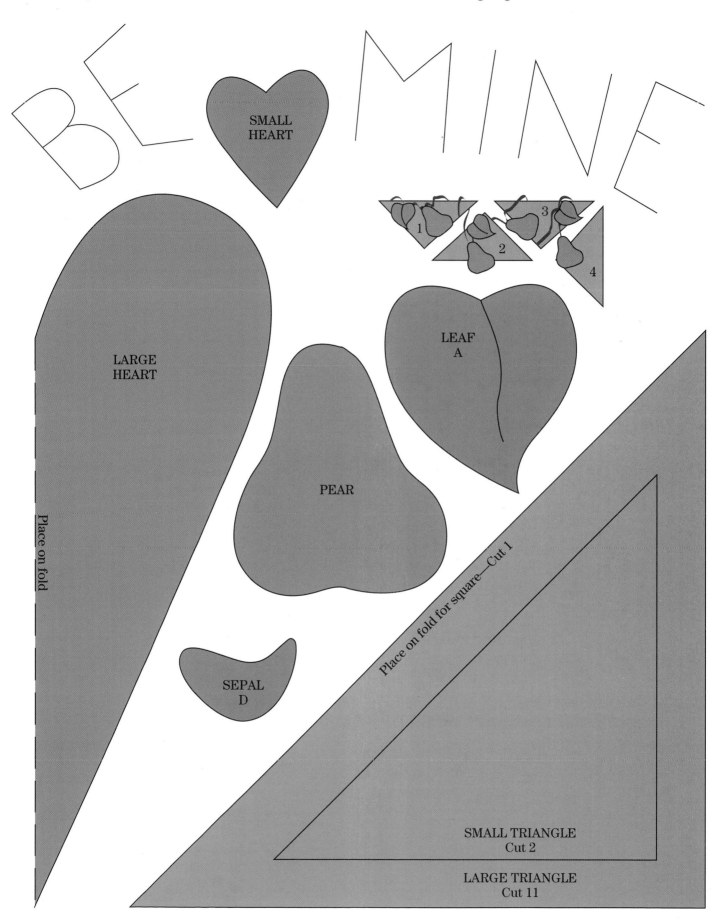

BE ♥ MINE

SMALL HEART

1 2 3 4

LARGE HEART

Place on fold

LEAF A

PEAR

SEPAL D

Place on fold for square—Cut 1

SMALL TRIANGLE
Cut 2

LARGE TRIANGLE
Cut 11

113

Forever Friends

The best thing about friendship is that it can last forever!

With heart in hand, the shy, demure bunny girl on the heart-shaped wool felt wallhanging, *below*, makes it easy to say, "Somebunny Loves You."

Here and on the following pages you'll find other sweet expressions of friendship such as the pin pals (they're bear and bunny heads

dressed in bonnets to wear on your lapel).

A delightful felt and fabric bear and bunny duo are shown *opposite*. Forever-friends—Miss Prim and Mrs. Proper—are all dressed up in their Sunday-best outfits trimmed with silk ribbon and bits of lace. These charming companions are taking time to enjoy a hot cup of tea, fancy flowers, and friendship.

"SOMEBUNNY LOVES YOU" WALLHANGING

Wallhanging is 24" high x 17" wide

For information about the materials, tools, techniques, and stitches, read "Tips and Techniques" starting on page 7.

Materials

¾ yard of 72"-wide blue spruce wool felt for the large heart and cuffs

¾ yard of 72"-wide straw wool felt for the center heart, banner, and backing

One 9" x 12" piece of either camel, champagne or beige wool felt for the head, hands, and feet

One 9" x 12" piece or scrap of light plum wool felt for the small heart

One 9" x 22" piece of patchwork-print fabric for the dress and sleeves

1½ yards of ⅝"-wide ecru lace

Size 8 DMC pearl cotton: one ball each of black (No. 310), light beige (No. 822)

Size 5 DMC pearl cotton: one skein of dark blue-green (No. 500)

4mm YLI silk ribbon: one 5-yard reel of blue-green (No. 32)

No. 22 and No. 26 chenille needles

Brass charms: one bow, one heart

Mark-B-Gone marking pens: water-erasable or disappearing-ink

Prepare Pattern Pieces

1. Fold a 19" x 24" sheet of tracing paper in half lengthwise. With the fold of the paper placed on the foldline of the pattern and referring to the heart pattern diagram on page 126, trace the tops of the large and the center heart patterns on page 124 (the red lines). Matching A to A and B to B, trace the second portion of each heart pattern from page 125. Matching C to C and D to D, trace the third portion of each heart pattern from page 126. To complete the pattern, match E to E and F to F and trace the bottom of each heart from page 126. Cut out and unfold the paper for a complete pattern.

2. Fold another sheet of tracing paper in half. With the fold of the paper placed on the foldline of the banner pattern on page 126, trace the pattern, including the word "Somebunny". Cut out the banner pattern and unfold the paper for a complete pattern. Trace "Loves You!!!" on the opposite side of the tracing paper banner.

3. Trace the remaining full-size patterns on pages 124-125 and cut out.

Prepare Fabric Pieces

1. Shrink the wool felt, washing each color separately. Dry in dryer.

2. On blue spruce wool felt, trace around the large heart pattern; do not cut at this time. Trim the pattern along the center heart line. On straw wool felt, trace around the center heart and banner patterns. Cut out.

3. Use the pattern as a guide to hand-print the lettering on the banner using either a water-erasable or disappearing-ink marker.

4. For the dress appliqués, with right sides together, fold the fabric in half across the width. On the back of the folded fabric, trace one dress and two sleeves.

Machine-sew the two layers of fabric together, stitching right on the traced lines. Cut out, adding a very narrow seam allowance. Carefully cut a slit in the back of each piece, then turn each piece right side out through its slit. Press. (If preferred, cut away the back layer so only a ¼" seam remains on the back.)

5. Using blue-green silk ribbon, embroider random lines on the dress and sleeves.

6. From scraps of blue spruce felt, cut two cuffs. From light plum wool felt, cut one small heart. From beige wool felt, cut one head, two hands, and each foot.

Stitch the Design

1. Pin the center heart to the large heart. Arrange lace trim along the edge of the center heart, overlapping the ends at the inner point. Trim off the excess.

   Attach the straight edge of the lace with blue-green pearl cotton and a running stitch. Along the scalloped edge, tack the point of each scallop in place with light beige pearl cotton.

2. Use blue-green pearl cotton to stem-stitch the phrase "Somebunny Loves You!!!" on the banner.

   Cut out the banner. Referring to the photo for placement, pin the banner to the large heart and blanket-stitch in place with blue-green pearl cotton.

3. With black pearl cotton, embroider the bunny's nose and eyes. The dots show where the whiskers will be added later.

4. Arrange the bunny on the center heart. The dashed lines on the patterns show where the pieces overlap.

5. With silk ribbon and the No. 26 needle, attach the cuffs with running stitches.

6. With light beige pearl cotton, blanket-stitch all exposed edges of the head and feet in place.

After I made this heart-shaped wallhanging, it was easier than ever to say "Somebunny Loves You!"

7. With black pearl cotton, blanket-stitch all exposed edges of the dress and sleeves in place.

8. For the whiskers, thread a needle with light beige pearl cotton. Insert the needle at one dot on the bunny's nose and come out at a dot on the opposite side of the nose. Leaving a long tail on each side of the face, remove the needle and trim the pearl cotton so that each whisker measures about 1¾". Repeat this step so there are three whiskers on each side of the face.

9. With blue-green pearl cotton, blanket-stitch around the edges of the small heart. Add a pearl cotton loop to the top of the heart and tack it between the bunny's hands. Sew a button to the top of the heart and a heart-shaped charm just below the button.

Finish the Wallhanging

1 Cut out the large heart. Use this as a pattern to cut out a matching piece of straw wool felt for the backing.

2. Place the stitched piece right side up on the backing, and blanket-stitch them together with blue-green pearl cotton.

3. With silk ribbon, attach the bow-shaped charm below the bunny's neck.

4. Apply cosmetic blush to the bunny's cheeks, toes, and the inside of each ear.

5. Thread a needle with a 12" length of silk ribbon. Take a stitch at the top of the bunny's head between her ears, leaving two long tails. Tie a bow.

BUNNY AND BEAR PINS
Bunny pin is about 4½" high
Bear pin is about 3" high with hat

For information about the materials, tools, techniques, and stitches, read "Tips and Techniques" starting on page 7.

Materials
One 9" x 12" piece of straw wool felt for the two heads

♥

One 9" x 12" piece each or scraps of light plum and blue spruce wool felt for the hats

♥

Size 5 DMC pearl cotton: one skein or scraps of black (No. 310)

♥

Size 8 DMC pearl cotton: one ball or scraps of light beige (No. 822)

♥

No. 22, No. 24, and No. 26 chenille needles

♥

Black E-beads for the eyes

♥

One 1" pin-back for each pin

♥

Polyester stuffing

♥

Mark-B-Gone water-erasable marking pen

♥

FOR THE BUNNY'S HAT
2mm YLI silk ribbon (C): one 5-yard reel each of green (No. 20), ecru (No. 156)

♥

7mm YLI silk ribbon (B): one 5-yard reel of pink rose (No. 127)

♥

FOR THE BEAR'S HAT
2mm YLI silk ribbon (C): one 5-yard reel each of yellow (No. 15), green (No. 20), blue (No. 45), ecru (No. 156), light grape (No. 178)

♥

4mm YLI silk ribbon (A): one 5-yard reel each of dark dusty rose (No. 114), dark burgundy (No. 137)

♥

Heads
1. From page 122, trace the full-size head and muzzle patterns. Trace the full-size hat patterns, opposite. Cut out.
2. Fold straw wool felt in half. On doubled felt, trace one head and one muzzle for each pin, leaving enough space between pieces to allow for seam allowances.
3. Machine-sew on the traced lines, beginning and ending all stitching with a backstitch. Do not leave an opening on heads. Leave muzzles open as marked.
4. Cut out pieces, leaving a narrow seam allowance and cutting the open edge of muzzle on the traced line; turn. Turn in raw edges ¼" and insert stuffing.
5. On one side of each head, cut a slit where face will be covered by muzzle; turn right side out. With light beige pearl cotton, cross-stitch through both layers along the base of each ear (see patterns).
6. Stuff the heads. Hand-sew slits closed. Hand-sew a muzzle to each face, covering the slit.
7. With black pearl cotton, satin-stitch the nose. Add bead eyes.

Bear Hat
1. From the blue spruce wool felt, cut two hat pieces.
2. Referring to the stitch guide, use No. 26 chenille needle to embroider flower design on front of one hat piece.
3. Place embroidered hat piece, right side up, on top of unstitched hat piece. Sew together with 2mm ecru silk ribbon and running stitches.

Forever Friends

Bunny Hat

1. From light plum wool felt, cut one hat piece. Use this as a pattern to cut a second hat piece, adding ¼" to ½" along the top edge.
2. Referring to the stitch guide, use No. 24 and 26 chenille needles to embroider silk ribbon roses on smaller hat piece.
3. Place embroidered hat piece on top of unstitched hat piece, matching the bottom edges. Sew together along top edge of embroidered piece, using 2mm ecru silk ribbon and running stitches. Repeat the running stitches along the top edge of larger piece.
4. Thread needle with 2mm green ribbon. Weave green ribbon in and out of the running stitches as seen on pattern.

Finish Hats

1. Turning under the bottom raw edge about ¼", wrap a hat around each head and hand-sew to back of head. Hand-sew a pin-back to back of each head.

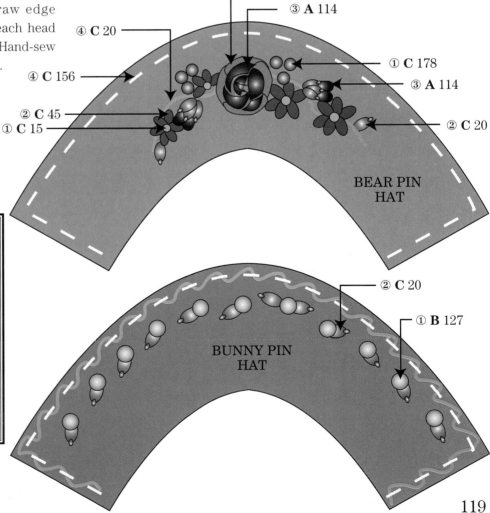

③ A 137
③ A 114
④ C 20
④ C 156
① C 178
③ A 114
② C 45
① C 15
② C 20

BEAR PIN HAT

② C 20
① B 127

BUNNY PIN HAT

STITCHES

① French Knot Stitch
(page 12)
② Lazy Daisy Stitch
(page 12)
③ Bullion Stitch
(page 11)
④ Running Stitch
(page 12)

119

BUNNY AND BEAR DOLLS

Dolls are from 12" to 14" tall

For information about materials, tools, techniques, and stitches, read "Tips and Techniques" starting on page 7.

Materials

¼ yard of straw wool felt for the two bodies, two heads, two muzzles, and four arms

♥

¼ yard of blue spruce wool felt for four legs, and the bear's coat and hat

♥

Two 9" x 12" pieces of light plum wool felt for the bunny's coat

♥

Scraps of burgundy wool felt for the bear's heart

♥

Scraps of loden wool felt for the leaves on bear's coat

♥

One 7½" x 13" piece of cotton print fabric for each skirt

♥

One 7" x 11½" piece of cotton print fabric for each underskirt

♥

⅓ yard of ¾" to 1"-wide ecru lace trim for each underskirt

♥

Size 5 DMC pearl cotton: one skein of black (No. 310)

♥

Size 8 DMC pearl cotton: one ball or scraps of light beige (No. 822)

♥

No. 22, No. 24, and No. 26 chenille needles

♥

Black E-beads for the eyes

♥

Doll needle

♥

Polyester stuffing

♥

Mark-B-Gone water-erasable marking pen

♥

FOR THE BEAR

2mm YLI silk ribbon (C): one 5-yard reel of green (No. 20)

♥

4mm YLI silk ribbon (A): one 5-yard reel of dusty rose (No. 113)

♥

7mm YLI silk ribbon (B): one 5-yard reel of burgundy (No. 129)

♥

Five white ⅜" buttons

♥

⅓ yard of gold-nugget color Offray 2mm chainette

♥

FOR THE BUNNY

4mm YLI silk ribbon: one reel each or scraps of light yellow (No. 13), dusty rose (No. 113)

♥

One white ⁷⁄₁₆" shank button

♥

½ yard of antique crocheted lace

♥

Dolls

1. Trace the full-size patterns onto tracing paper. Cut out.
2. Referring to instructions for bear and bunny pins on page 118, make one bunny and one bear head. Set aside.
3. With water-erasable marking pen, trace around body pattern twice and arm pattern four times on doubled straw wool felt, leaving enough space between pieces to allow for seam allowances. In the same way, trace four legs on doubled blue spruce felt.
4. Leaving openings as marked, machine-sew on the traced lines, beginning and ending all seams with a backstitch.

5. Cut out, leaving narrow seam allowances. Turn each piece right side out. Insert stuffing. Turn in raw edges and hand-sew openings closed.

6. Referring to the body pattern, mark dots on each side of two bodies. On each arm and leg, mark a dot ¼" below the straight edge.

7. Thread the doll needle with light beige pearl cotton and knot the end. Insert needle at upper dot on one side of body and come out at dot on opposite side of body. Insert needle through one arm at the dot and go back through arm a short distance from this dot.

 Next, draw needle back through body coming out at starting point and add second arm. Bring needle back through arm a short distance from dot and tie off thread at starting point. Attach legs at lower dots in same way.

8. Hand-sew the head of the bear or the bunny to the body at the neck, sewing the back of the head to the front of the neck, overlapping ½".

Skirts

1. For each underskirt, press under a ½" hem along each 11½" edge. Sew the lace trim to one 11½" edge. With the right sides together, sew 7" edges for the center back seam.

2. Thread needle with a doubled strand of light beige pearl cotton. Hand-sew a line of running stitches around waist edge, starting and ending stitching at center front and leaving a long tail at each end. Place underskirt on doll. Gather waist edge to fit doll and tie a bow.

3. For each skirt, sew two 7½" edges with right sides together. Press under a ½" hem at the waist edge and bottom edge.

 Thread needle with a single strand of light beige pearl cotton and hand-sew the hem at the bottom of skirt with long running stitches. Gather and fit waist as

for the underskirt, positioning skirt so lace of underskirt shows.

Coats

1. From blue spruce felt, cut two coat pieces. Trim length of pattern at cutting line for the bunny's coat, and cut two light plum coat pieces. Unfold each coat piece and mark the dots at each shoulder seam.

2. Sew coat together at shoulders, leaving open between dots. Sew the underarm and side seams. Clip underarm seams; turn. Cut front open along fold line. Gather neck opening. Place the coat on the doll, pulling gathers to fit.

Finish Bunny

1. Dress bunny in light plum coat. Cut lace to fit around each wrist. Attach lace with light yellow ribbon and running stitches, tying the ends together in a bow.

2. With light yellow ribbon, gather remaining lace to fit around bunny's neck; tie ends together in a bow.

3. Fold an 18" length of dusty rose ribbon in half and pull one end through back of a small shank button. Tie a bow behind button; wrap ribbon around bunny's head below ears. Tie ends in back; tack in place.

Finish Bear

1. From blue spruce felt, cut two hat pieces, two cuffs, and one collar. From burgundy felt cut two hearts. From loden felt, cut four leaves.

2. Referring to the stitch guide, opposite, use Nos. 24 and 26 chenille needles to embroider the front of one hat piece and the collar, attaching small leaves.

3. Place embroidered hat piece on top of unstitched hat and sew together with 2mm green ribbon and running stitches. Turning under the bottom raw edge about ¼", wrap the hat around bear's head and hand-sew to back of head.

4. Wrap a cuff around each wrist. Where ends overlap, hand-sew a button in place, at the same time sewing cuff to the sleeve.

5. Wrap collar around bear's neck. Hand-sew in place with a small button; add buttons to front of coat.

6. Place hearts together; stitch design through both layers. Fold chainette in half. Holding the fold in one hand, use a needle to bring the two loose ends to front of heart, leaving tails long enough to tie into a bow.

   Hand-sew the bear's hands together, catching folded end of chainette in the stitches.

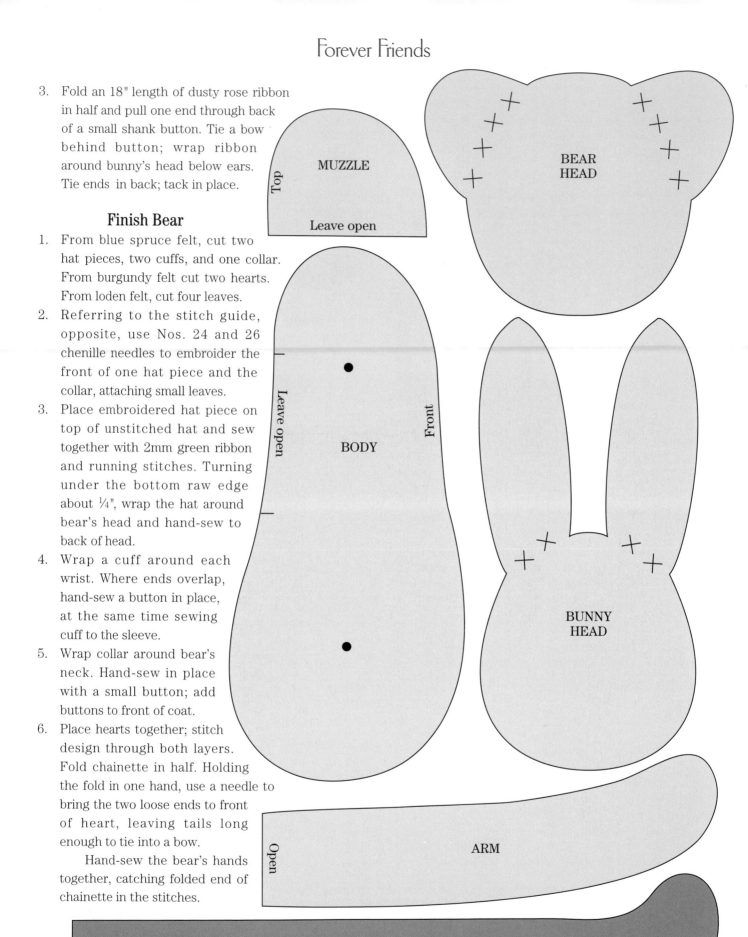

Forever Friends

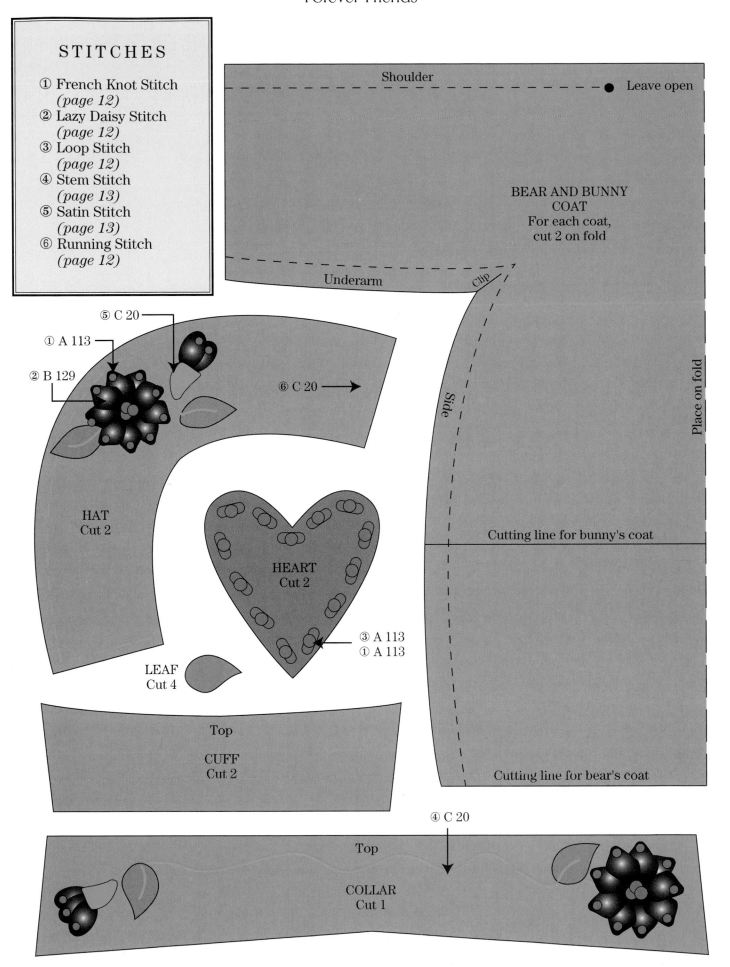

STITCHES

① French Knot Stitch
(page 12)
② Lazy Daisy Stitch
(page 12)
③ Loop Stitch
(page 12)
④ Stem Stitch
(page 13)
⑤ Satin Stitch
(page 13)
⑥ Running Stitch
(page 12)

Shoulder   ● Leave open

BEAR AND BUNNY
COAT
For each coat,
cut 2 on fold

Underarm   Clip

Side

Place on fold

⑤ C 20
① A 113
② B 129

⑥ C 20 →

HAT
Cut 2

HEART
Cut 2

③ A 113
① A 113

Cutting line for bunny's coat

LEAF
Cut 4

Top

CUFF
Cut 2

Cutting line for bear's coat

④ C 20

Top

COLLAR
Cut 1

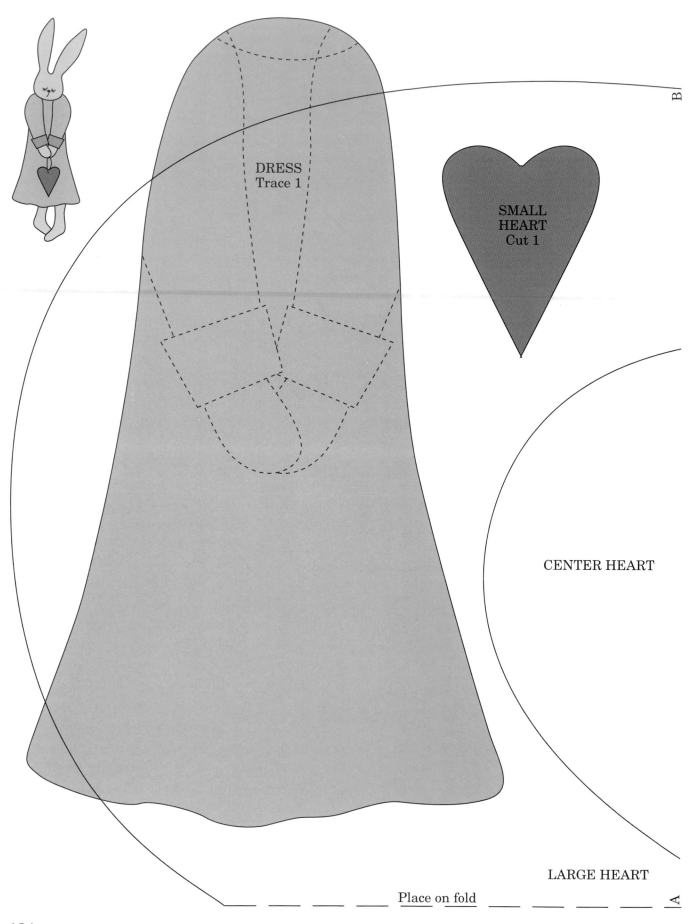

B

DRESS
Trace 1

SMALL
HEART
Cut 1

CENTER HEART

LARGE HEART

Place on fold

A

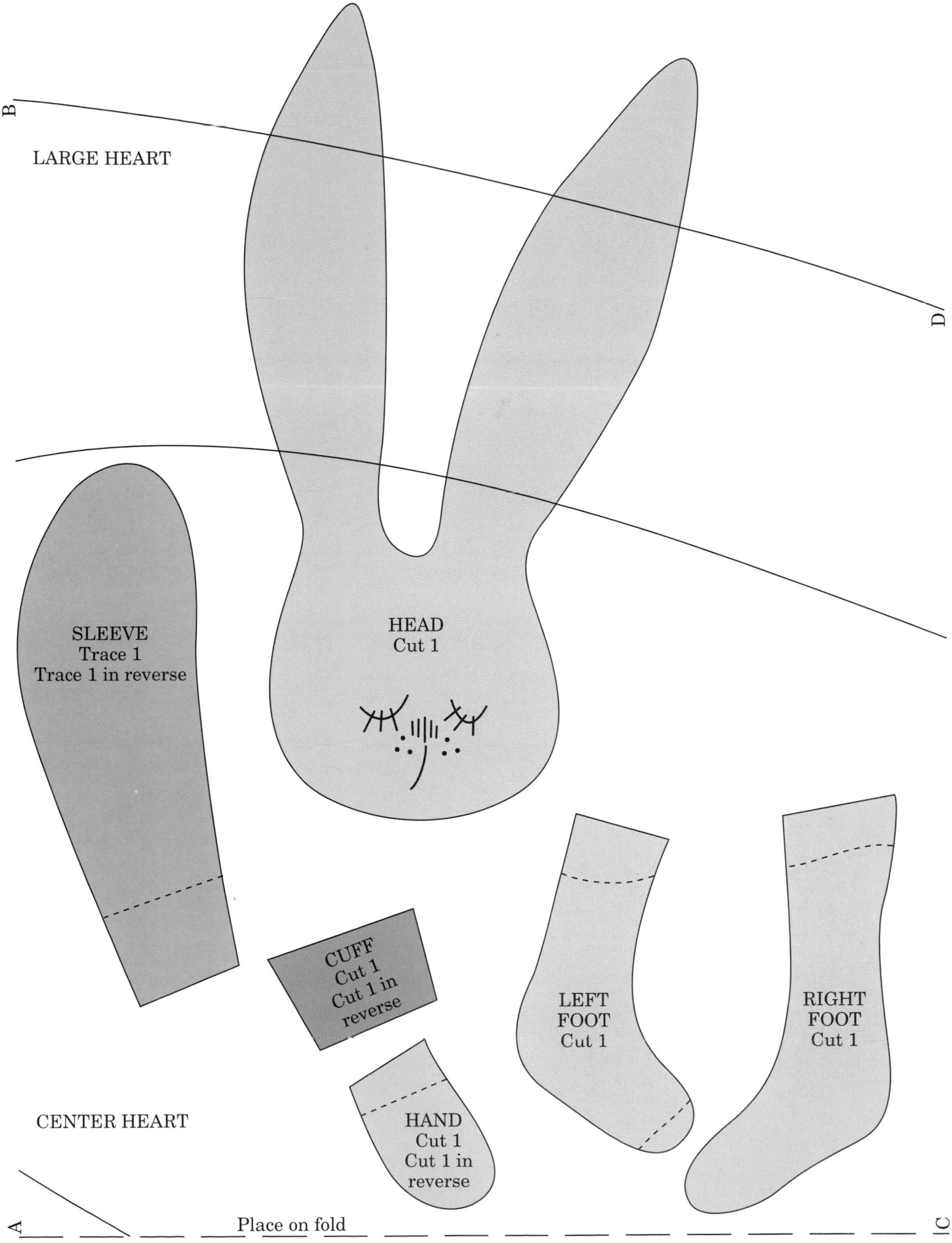

B

LARGE HEART

D

SLEEVE
Trace 1
Trace 1 in reverse

HEAD
Cut 1

CUFF
Cut 1
Cut 1 in
reverse

LEFT
FOOT
Cut 1

RIGHT
FOOT
Cut 1

HAND
Cut 1
Cut 1 in
reverse

CENTER HEART

A

Place on fold

C

BANNER
Cut 1 on fold

Foldline

D

LARGE HEART

LARGE
HEART

CENTER
HEART

B

D

F

A   C   E

Heart pattern diagram

F

F

LARGE HEART

CENTER HEART

E   Place on fold

C

Place on fold

E